The Golem of Los Angeles

The Golem of Los Angeles

Poems

❧

Tony Barnstone

for Sweet Cherry,
The Indiana fruit is
green rain through leaves, thoughts
coursing through limestone
caves underground, an old wood
cabin in the forest inhabited

RED HEN PRESS | LOS ANGELES, CALIFORNIA

by your lovely spirit, and
you! with love,

The Golem of Los Angeles

Book design by Mark E. Cull

ISBN: 978-1-59709-098-8
Library of Congress Catalog Card Number: 2007938216

The City of Los Angeles Department of Cultural Affairs, Los Angeles County Arts Commission, California Arts Council and the National Endowment for the Arts partially support Red Hen Press.

Red Hen Press
www.redhen.org

First Edition

Acknowledgments

The Golem of Los Angeles was a finalist for the Dorsett Prize, 2005, the Philip Levine Prize in Poetry, 2005, the May Swenson Poetry Prize, 2005 and 2006, the 2nd Annual Robert E. Lee & Ruth I. Wilson Poetry Book Award, 2005, the Ashland Poetry Prize, 2005, and the Prairie Schooner Book Prize in Poetry, 2004; it was a runner-up for the Cleveland State University Poetry Center Open Competition, 2005 and the Main Street Rag Chapbook Contest, 2002; and it was a semi-finalist for the Ohio State University Press/The Journal Award in Poetry, 2006, the Kathryn A. Morton Prize in Poetry, 2005 and the Brittingham Prize, 2004 and 2006. "Parable of the Jew without a Name" won 2nd place in the St. Louis Poetry Center Prize in Poetry, 2004, and "Testament of the Oldest White Belt at the Tae Kwon Do Tournament" was a finalist for the *Indiana Review*'s "1/2 K" Prize for Prose Poems/Short-Shorts, 2004. Poems from the book have been nominated for the Pushcart Prize seven times, and "The 167th Psalm of Elvis" won a Pushcart Prize in 2006.

The following poems have appeared in the journals and anthologies listed, often in earlier versions.

Bear Flag Republic: Prose Poems and Poetics from California, edited by Christopher Buckley and Gary Young, Alcatraz Editions, 2007: "Parable of the Cracked Man," "Parable of the Burning House," "Psalm of Speed," "Parable of Aladdin in Oakland," and "Parable of the Hunter"; *Blood to Remember: American Poets on the Holocaust*, edited by Charles Fishman, Time Being Books, 2007: "Parable of the Jew without a Name"; *New Works Review*: "Psalm of Snow," "Psalm of Lucifer"; *Margie*: "Parable of the Jew without a Name"; *Measure*: "Discourse on Love in the Ruins," "Discourse on the Crippled God"; *The Cortland Review*: "Discourse of Roses," "Concerning Homographs," "In Which He Feels Aftereffects"; *Inkwell*: "Parable of the South Pole Buddha"; *The Evansville Review*: "Parable of Microphobia"; *The Pushcart Prize Anthology, 2006*: "The 167th Psalm of Elvis"; *Runes: Signals, 2005*: "The 167th Psalm of Elvis"; *Indiana Review*: "Parable of the Oldest White Belt at the Tae Kwon Do Tournament"; *Guernica*: "Parable of Greece, Grasshopper, Time"; *CrossXConnect*: "The Dead God Codex" and "The Suckee, Fuckee, Blowjob Sutra"; *Prairie Schooner*: "Gospel of the Golem of Los Angeles" and "Parable of the Birds"; *The Diagram*: "Gospel of Henry David Thoreau at the Circle K Convenience Store," "The California Book of the Dead" and "Discourse on the Crippled God"; *Poetry International*: "Parable on the Phenomenology of Childhood in Indiana" and "Gospel of the Famous Heart"; *The North American Review*: "Parable of the Nude Model"; *Artful Dodge*: "The Stone House Apocalypse"; *The Blue Moon Review*: "Parable of the Ancient Greek Urn" and "Parable of the Mummified Cat"; *Luna*: "The

Black Flower Sutra" and "Parable in Praise of Violence"; *Eclipse*: "Parable of Houdini's Last Show" and "Riding the Crotch Rocket"; *The Salt Journal*: "On Being a Man"; *The Drunken Boat*: "On Being a Man" and "The Mirror Psalm"; *Faultline*: "Coming in to Los Angeles" and "Drinking at the Well"; *Red Rock Review*: "Parable of the Gifts," "The Video Arcade Psalm," "Discourse on the Tao of Shoe Shopping," "Psalm of Climbing with Ghosts," "Coming in to Los Angeles," "In Simi Valley," "Azusa Boulevard," "Mirror Psalm," "Riding the Crotch Rocket," "Discourse on Saying No" and "In Which He Goes to Hear Some Blue Jazz"; *Sierra Nevada College Review*: "Terminal Testament"; *Poemeleon*: "Concerning a Bag of Potato Chips," "Concerning Ghosts," "Concerning Lazarus at the Taverna," "Concerning the Great Rift Valley," "Concerning Birding at Lake Baringo" and "Concerning Malaria Dreams"; *The Formalist*: "Discourse on the Sunset as a Hermeneutic Cycle" and "Parable of the Found Objects (Pablo Picasso, 1945)"; *Knockout*: "Parable of the Burning House"; *The Pedestal Magazine* and the Poets Against the War website: "Parable of Aladdin in Oakland." The following poems first appeared in a chapbook titled *Naked Magic* (Main Street Rag Press, 2002): "The 167th Psalm of Elvis," "Parable of Houdini's Last Show," "Parable of Aladdin in Oakland," "The Gospel of Teen Jesus," "Spell for Balancing Stones," "Spell against Disease," "The Virgin Sutra," "Parable of the Gifts," "Discourse on Love in the Ruins," "The Stone House Apocalypse," "Parable of the Mummified Cat," "Parable of an Ancient Greek Urn," "Parable of the Nude Model," "Parable of the Cracked Man," "Discourse on the Tao of Shoe Shopping," "Parable of Microphobia," "Parable of in Praise of Violence," "The Black Flower Sutra."

A number of the following poems were displayed in a sculpture installation titled "The Narrative Forest." The Narrative Forest is a series of twenty-four stainless steel plates laser-etched with poetry and mounted on cedar stands, designed and built by the sculptor and architect Robert Barnstone, and including eight poems each by me, by Aliki Barnstone and by Willis Barnstone. This award-winning project was on display for a year at the Convergences for the Arts festival in Providence, R.I., and has been on display for several years at Whittier College.

Many thanks to friends and family who have supported me during the writing of this book: Willis Barnstone, Elli Barnstone, Aliki Barnstone, Robert Barnstone, Sholeh Wolpé, Alan Michael Parker, Christopher Bakken, Charles Harper Webb, Richard Garcia, William Baer, Alicia Stallings, Louise Mathias, John Fitzgerald, Hélène Cardona, Britni Sternquist, Shannon Phillips, Melissa Onstad, Dawn Finley, Mark Turpin, Sharon May, Dan Weiss, Andrea Troyer, Charmaine Craig, J. J. Webb, Brian Turner, Elena Byrne, Caley O'Dwyer, Tom Babayan, Thomas Yuill, Tim Fuller, Kevin Greene, Ayame Fukuda and Caroline Heldman.

This book is for Caley O'Dwyer and Tom Babayan

Contents

TURTLE HEAD GOSPELS

The Book of Elvis

The 167ᵗʰ Psalm of Elvis

Blessed are the marble breasts of Venus,
those ancient miracles, for they are upright and milk white
and they point above the heads of the crowd in the casino.
Blessed are the crowds that play, and whose reflections
sway in the polish of her eggshell eyes,
for they circle like birds around the games,
and they are beautiful and helpless.
Bless the fast glances that handle the waitress,
bless her miniskirt toga and the flame-gold scotch,
and bless the gamblers who gaze at the stage.
Remember also the dancer and remember her dance,
her long neck arched like a wild white goose,
the tassels on her nipples that shoot like sparks,
and bless the legs and bless the breasts
for they are fruit and honey and they are generous to the eyes.
Have mercy on my wallet, the dollars I punch into the slot,
and grace the wheels swapping clubs and hearts.
Mercy on me too, as I stumble as if in a hashish haze
watching the reels spin away, for I am a blown fuse
and I need someone to bless me before it's too late.
Honor the chance in a million, the slot machine jolting,
the yellow light flashing, honor the voice that calls *jackpot,*
and the coins that crush into the brushed steel tray,
for there is a time for winning and a time for losing
and if you cast your bread upon the waters
you will find it again after many days.
Pity the crowd around the blessed winner
all patting his back as if it rubs off,
this juice, this force, this whatever

that might save them from their own cursed luck.
And pity the poor winner whose hand claws back
into his bucket of coins and who cannot walk away,
because he'd do anything for the feeling he had
when the great pattern rose from the chaos
of cherries and lemons and diamonds and stars
and he knew for that moment he was blessed.

Parable of Microphobia

All day I battled ants, their tiny scrambling legs,
their plated armor crunching under my thumb, their endlessness.
A queen had made a hidden nest inside our fridge,
replicating behind the clean white surfaces,
but we didn't know the intimate electric works inside
were aswarm, wires alive with antic activity,
until the first small scouts emerged upon the tundra
of the freezer, Antarctic explorers
dark against the white continent of frost,
their brittle bodies found stuck to mountains
of frozen peas and pot stickers, so close to Paradise.
The first ones were a sign of things to come.
Like soldiers on the shore at Iwo Jima they crawled
through ducts and under rubber seals and came
to die in thousands against the food, a fur of bodies
frozen to the plastic barriers that kept them out.
And so I vacuumed up the corpses, plugged the holes
with caulk and put out poison they refused to eat,
and still they broke into the treasure box and died.
And now in bed I'm antsy, knowing they're still crawling
out of crevices to perish by my perishables,
and so I scratch my head and slap my face and drift away
at last watching them crawl down my lids like teeny herds
of sheep and take residence inside my skull,
their slender legs, their eating mouths, their endlessness.

The Virgin Sutra

I didn't even know not to bite my nails, but to keep them bright,
intact, convex, elastic, and polished in appearance,
to press her skin so softly it leaves no mark, but scratches out
a teeny sound and leaves the hair erect, like metal shavings magnetized.

If I did I could have made half moons on her neck,
impressed moon circles on the small cavities above the butt,
made a tiger's claw or peacock's foot on the breast,
or scratched her hip with five marks like a blue lotus leaf.

Instead, I came to Eric's door and she opened up and said,
Come in, take off your clothes, and I did, and then sweaty,
fumbling, we were having sex on the couch, and I was zooming
out into that sportscaster's position far above the stadium,

observing, *He's just a rookie, he's just not very good at this yet.*
Sure, later I would learn about biting just enough to redden the skin,
about the wild boar rub, mounting of a horse, the tiger jump and elephant press.
And I haven't even mentioned the sucking of the mango.

But on that day, I just had sex for the first time, giving my body
away, and we were impossibly sweet and awkward, and we tried
to be good to each other. In those days sex didn't kill
and we thought the country could run on love as easily as on money,

with just a shift of mind. How foolish that seems in these plague times.
There was much we didn't know. Apparently there are things
you do to the penis, such as rubbing it with the bristles
of certain insects that live in trees or with the fruit

of the eggplant, the butter of a she buffalo, or with oil boiled
on a moderate fire along with pomegranate
and cucumber seeds. And who knew that the sweat
of the testicle of a white horse will make a blotched lip white?

But on that day, we were simply good to each other, had inept sex
and kissed each other tenderly, kissed as if the whole world
could be invited inside the house, lips and thighs kissing
on the couch, clumsily at first, it is hard to learn how to touch,

but soon getting the hang of it, the ghosts of the tortured dead
kissed back to life, child soldiers learning how to plug in
their souls, poets and acrobats learning how to sob
and leap, everyone together learning how to kiss.

Parable of Aladdin in Oakland

"Would you mind minding my store?"
asks the Persian woman in Piedmont Lighting,
and she's out the door in a breath
leaving me alone with giant lilies that bend
brushed steel necks long and tapered
as a swan's over a desk. I duck my head
so not to catch my hair in the solar system
dangling from the ceiling, blueberry and custard
planets, the halogen dwarfs and incandescent
giants, and soak in the brilliant milk of this
paradise of lamps. Here a standing lamp lifts
its burnished face, and here a reading light
concentrates on a book, and other shining eyes
bathe me with such gentle attention I feel
the bulbs of my eyes bloom light, as if someone
has flicked a switch and made everything I see
shimmer bright, releasing all the genies
with a single *Let there be light.*

I worry if the owner is all right
looking Persian on the street
in these days after the Twin Towers went up
in flames and then came down,
since people need someone to carry their blame.
These days it's hard not to worry
when it will all give out, our president
trying to stop fire with flame, the oil in our tanks
turning to cancer in our brains, the weapons waiting
underground in silos to give off their great light

and send the planet spinning through space
like a dead bulb towards a trashcan.
I think of all the lamps in this marvelous altar,
each one a luminous tongue giving out
a shout of praise, and wonder if the world
will end in fire. From what I've seen
I'd say it's just as like to end like this,
with a finger flipping a switch.

The Gospel of Teen Jesus

The art of yielding isn't hard to master,
and that's why he should not do acid.
He's the one who trips angelic and impassioned
at a concert, then walks into the wet air
to take a leak on the new-cut lawn and watch
the fuzzy awful starlight rotate overhead.
He has a knack for giving in to visions and delusions,
sharing joints with cartoon skeletons and pigs
by a gnarled and grumbling tangled root-mess
while the music rips him from his body,
electric arc discharged into the sweaty grass.

Now he leans on the railing of a bridge
above the tainted shallow creek the students call
the River Jordan, watching water passing
under, black glimmer of the small ripples
in the streetlights, and thinks that's what we are,
water between shores passing through.
That's what everything is, empty space
between electrons, just Buddha breath
and empty buildings everywhere, and if he lets go
enough to leap head first right off this bridge
he will not crack his nut against the world.

Now the music rises toward that harmony
that shatters glass and makes a bridge collapse.
Watch him raise his arms like a diver
and look up to the heavens where the spheres pivot
in some sudden, shining, singing vision

of a great and yellow sign that says to *Yield*.
He yields like water that parts for him like the Dead Sea.
He yields like the earth as he flies straight through
the limestone, geode, earthworm streambed,
condoms and trilobites, quarters and popsicle sticks,
through the chicken broth of nuclei and positrons,
into the very geothermal womb of the earth.

No, not true. He's still standing on the bridge
when the movie snaps. His knack for giving in,
for giving up on this world, for getting smashed
until he forgets to be, has torn a hole at the back
of his mind. He steps through it, feeling prophetic.

The Stone House Apocalypse

Red centipedes breed in the storage space
beneath the bed. One skitters at the edge of sight
then freezes on the white wall like a spatter of blood.
My wife shrieks but whacks it dead
with a flyswatter while I flutter
about the room in insect dread.

Roly-polies bumble up the walls, and small white ants
swarm in the sugar bowl.
At night we sleep with crawlies creeping up our legs
and fliers bashing against the net.
Even as I write now, I lift one hand from the keys
and crush a mosquito in midair.

Come morning it's time to check the septic tank,
and when Rob pries up the plate an underworld wings out,
a buzz and surge of gnats and black flies,
mosquitoes lashing air with their thin gauze,
so many tiny devils on tarry wings
pouring up and pricking us with tiny pitchforks.

Now it's really Armageddon, the windows thrown open
to sweep the house clean, slapping our own faces
and legs, dancing like large and clumsy gods
as we bring death and death
to the things breeding beneath,
and pour diesel into the tank to choke the eggs.

Afterwards, we sleep a bit better, though still
the undermind swarms and stings and imagines
small things gathering in dark places,
multiplying in cracks and drains,
waiting for the day when again they'll climb
into the light of the world we've made.

Psalm of Climbing with Ghosts

Halfway to the top something pulls and I stop
by this blue cast-iron gate in the whitewashed wall,
this gated neighborhood of very small marble houses.
Listening to cicadas scrape in the olive trees,
I trespass among the headstones and tombs,
feeling lucky to have limbs that move,
and I raise a ghost toast to the moon.
Now a tugging at my bowels, sun fading fast,
the way up unsure, but I pause a moment longer
by those houses of earth, damp single-bed rooms
with a burned out bulb, and think of
the strong man of the village who could lift
a motorcycle with one hand, or the walleyed baker
with his face smudged white with flour,
of the boys playing soccer by the church,
of the captain's three daughters,
each more beautiful than the next,
and all now dead, dead, dead
and underground and eaten by the earth.
I listen to the wind sift
through the trees and then lift off
to become atmosphere, just sky spilling
through sky, the way the moment I put down this pen
the lucid marble of this graveyard will lift off
into time, or remain here as I lift myself
up the mountain toward the white
village above. And as if I weren't lost,
as if it were possible to climb away

from death, I walk through the dark
toward the lights, where the tables are made,
and the families quarrel and serve
and eat the feast that's set before them
inside the thick stone walls.

Mountain Cemetery, Serifos, Greece

The Black Flower Sutra

I see bruise flowers along the inside
of her arm, some still black, others violet, rose
or yellow, and raise my eyebrows to ask.

My Spanish friend pulls her sleeve down.
This is in the bar of the Beijing Hotel.
Her husband is in the bathroom.

He comes back to the table, sees my eyes
flicker to the dark blossoms above his wrist,
and he tells me. Their doctor had said,

Stop, or in six months you'll drop dead.
Therefore, this ratty teaching gig in China.
No way in Beijing to get heroin.

He tells me this through a smog of black tobacco,
and I ask, *You're not giving those up, though?*
He looks at me a moment, eyes overcast.

They say cigarettes kill slowly, he says,
and takes long drag. He lets it out deliciously
and smiles, *But I'm in no hurry.*

The Gospel of Kimmy at the Little Temple Bar

It's New Year's at the Little Temple Bar
and dreadlocked Shakespeare's rapping to wild sax,
guitar, a deejay mixing tracks. The star
dancer is Kimmy who flames up like sex
then screams and writhes down to the floor, all muscles,
beauty and attitude. Somehow at midnight
she chooses me to kiss, both cheeks, and tousles
my hair and tears my glasses off. Good night
to worship beauty at the Temple, though
as Kimmy says, *I hate all men, I want*
to destroy all of them. I'll start with you!
I tell the barman, *Vodka tonic, double,*
then try to kiss her mouth. She says, *You can't,*
and dances off. Her torn tee shirt reads, *Trouble.*

Parable of the Birds

As in a horror movie, their glances fly at her,
and though she's covered up in cloth
they pluck her hems and stockings, prick
her arms and calves and beat against
her crotch and on her thighs like black wings
against glass, swooping up-skirt and down
her blouse. They snatch her hair to wrap
the thoughts of breast and ass that nest
inside their brains. And say she catch gazes
on her nipples and she frowns; they'll snap
her lips up in their beaks. And say she steels
herself and tries to stare them down;
they'll steal her eyes like rings and fly away.

Parables of the Book

Parable of the Burning House

We could have burned to death in our sleep,
my roommate says, then brightly asks will I drive her
to the edge of town to see the flames
bounding through grass and up eucalyptus trees,
each tree a torch that lights the next so it relays itself
across the landscape into the hills above our house,
a river of black smoke roiling overhead,
splitting the sky into blue halves.
We drive to the park, where a little crowd
watches blazes lope through the valley then leap
the freeway towards us like yellow lions.
I am still in my head, thinking of Heraclitus,
the fire philosopher, who says all things are made
of fire and will change back into fire,
but when a light voice asks, *Mommy, is our house*
going to burn down again? and a heat-blast
prickles our cheeks, I shout, *Let's get out of here!*
and we ricochet to the car in cartoonish fear.

It's easy to talk about the baptism of fire,
about the forge of the spirit, the purifying flame,
but when the sun is a bloodshot planet in the smoke
and the sky fills with orange nebulae,
people watching on porches start to run.
When we get home, my roommate packs and flees
but I'm on the roof with the garden hose
watering the house down as fire spills downhill
into the graveyard across the street, the trees like brushes
painting the sky red above the sleeping dead.

I'm gauging how much time I have
before I must run, too, when the wind shifts
and I stand on the roof with the limp hose, watching,
guilty, relieved, as other peoples' houses burn.

Here is a woman riding out of the hills on the handlebars
of a young man's bicycle while her house flames behind.
Wait, she says, *my novel is in the house.*
It is ten years' work, no other copies,
but the young man doesn't understand.
Don't worry, he says, *it's only things.*
California is burning and it makes the eye burn,
the nose burn, the tongue burn, and as the matter
of the world goes up it makes the mind burn as well,
since all things of the world are on fire, with the fire
of lust, fire of suffering, fire of attachment.
But it isn't easy to be a Buddha and let go
of the world that houses our things, the mind
that houses the world, of the women who loved me
for a while, of even these words for which
I've had such hopes. It isn't easy at all,
and even if it were, what would be the point of being
that free, of standing alone when the fires die,
like this bathtub on claw feet in black stubble,
this field of chimneys without houses?

—For Maxine Hong Kingston

34

Parable of the Nude Model

The artists scribble furiously at the white inside
of my thigh to get the precise curl of my pubic hair
before the pose is up, my naked body
on the platform sexless as a marble torso,
an architecture of muscle and bone,
or so I am told. But that's crap, of course.
Sometimes after session I'm approached
by middle-aged men who want to compliment my *form*,
and I have trouble myself—tonight they've posed me
next to a woman from Russian literature class,
and as sweat shivers in the fine blond hairs above her lip
and the small chocolate bumps on her aureoles
scorch my pupils, my electric senses awake,
forces rip through me in waves
and my nihilist penis threatens to shatter creation.
What does a volt care about social order?
What does a wave care about propriety?
Shouldn't I stand up arrogant as poor doomed
Bazarov, as murderously proud as Raskolnikov?
But no, I keep the swelling down
with a drab reiteration of multiplication
tables and the conjugation of Spanish verbs,
and lapse back into being
a model man by a model of a woman,
once again turning into art—as if
the audience were only watching
these planes arranged in light and shade,
a gesture that runs through the limbs like water,
and not this cock and chest, the violence
of these sweet breasts glazed in sweat.

Parable of the Jew without a Name

"With our despised immigrant clothing, we shed also
our impossible Hebrew names."

—Mary Antin, *The Promised Land* (1912)

My great uncle Vincent, son of the Milk Street tailor,
threw some fairy dust into the air and changed,
making it easy for me to go to the prom,
to grow up in Indiana and bite my tongue
when a hick would cuss at *the bastard who tried*
to Jew me down on the price for homegrown pot.
Like wool pants for blue jeans, Moshe, Shmuel and Lazar
traded in their names, and in exchange were changed
from cabbage-eaters into Americans, and why not?
"I never was a pumpkin!" cries the carriage.
"I never was a pauper!" shouts the prince.
In this fairy tale all the steins turn into stones, straw turns
to gold, stars warp into crosses, and the pauper trades up
and leaves the trades to the star-crossed Jews.

I'm a lousy Jew, ignorant of nearly everything
except that in another time the Klan would lynch me,
the Nazis flay me into yellow lampshades.
My white hide hides me, my baseball cap keeps greasy ash
out of my hair, and I'm glad for my nice name.
Who needs a life so grim? In the shtetl, the old Jews
would change their names so the Angel of Death
flying on black crape wings above the town,
fatal list in hand, would pass over them
—but not the ones who stayed behind
and kept their names, the Adelsteins, Eisensteins

or the one I'll never know, some cousin twice removed
born in Poland, some Maurice Bernstein. No way to gather
smoke out of the sky and give him flesh again.

I imagine him, with eyes like mine, intent
and studious, staring at the rusted cattle-car wall
in the rattling stink of packed bodies, trying not to breathe.
He'll get that wish soon enough.
Slender, bookish children aren't good workers
and it's too much trouble to take away their names
and write numbers in their skin.
They're gassed like fleas.
I'm a lousy Jew, but I'd like to disturb the grass,
unearth him from the crowded grave, and let his damp fingers
write this story, while his eyes like clouded marble roll.
I'd like to roll the story back to the dead boy
swaying in the train, to see him there imagining the sky
he hasn't seen for days, the white winter sky, like a page
he could write on again and again, practicing his name.

Parable of the Cracked Man

The homeless man in Starbucks argues wildly
with himself in a woofer-without-tweeter voice,
an incoherent bass wave that startles students
from Berkeley who've come with fold-up wooden
book holders to cram for exams in the pleasant wash of talk
and roasted reek of coffee, milk-steam, chocolate dust.
They sure didn't expect this growling bass guitar
of addled humanity staring avuncularly into the middle air
where the Devil is supposed to dwell, Prince of Air
and pride and lies, man of a thousand faces, the Lon Chaney
of the Medieval theater; they sure didn't expect
the black tobacco and night sweat and shit and poverty
and pure crazy street living blended into this foul
and strangely sweet reek, exotic as rotting tamarinds;
and so the blond woman studying law rolls her eyes
dramatically toward the door and her Asian boyfriend
slams his textbook shut with a gunshot *crack*,
and they edge carefully between the window
and the back of his woolen army coat, leaving him
at the long wooden table drawing angles and loops
and equations on a scattering of blue lined sheets.
I note his blue ballpoint, crabbed notes on the notebook
pages spread before him, coded spirals and points
of intersection, the fractured math, milk froth
on his bearded chin, and see he's here to study too,
that the dead eyes fixed on nothing are not
disconnected from the sea roar of the voice
and the blotched body hunched within the army jacket.
What microscopic fright would the biologist have to see

in his tiny glass; what depth would the lawyer
have to fall to in his RayBans and Italian shoes;
what sort of test would you have to bomb to end up
this damaged, this foul, mumbling and staring
at some geometry of horror while the mouth articulates
basso profondo that freeway rumble, that music of disaster,
ocean waves bursting and pulling the world under?

Parable on the Phenomenology of Childhood in Indiana

Old friend, you write, *Why write? It's all trash,*
nothing to say. Maybe you're right. Why keep writing
with this tool to inscribe time, line by line, measuring
what is lost as it leaves? No one reads this stuff.

If only the words were a body I could inhabit
and you could feel me through this membrane,
like skins touching. I remember one day telling you
I felt I was just starting to wake from the long dumb

sleep of childhood, but was lost in the dark rush
of the senses, and I imagined my spirit
as a blind reaching through flesh and tickertape
consciousness, a hand trying to grasp itself.

I would like to believe in souls reaching through
the flesh for understanding, hungry to be seen
and detecting each other through defective means.
I would like to believe this life is a sleep we'll wake from,

that some conductor drives our spirits through
this tunnel and for a reason. But I find myself talking
in darkness, huddled around the narrow flame
of my own being, the way a child I knew (yes, me)

would walk home from the bus stop chanting nonsense
because when he fell silent the empty dark
closed in and made him know how blind he was,
how ravenous for dinner, lights, and mother.

And he would make the television blaze and shout
just to stop that dead black eye from staring.
And in bed, he'd pull the covers over his head
when his mother said, *Lights out,* and pray for sleep.

Parable of the Ancient Greek Urn

An ancient Greek urn swollen with barnacles, pulled from the sand's suck. For centuries the sea clothed the clay with seashells. Who could imagine this urn would surface on the other side of time, grotesque and beautiful? I rinse it in the surf, buff it with a beach towel, hoping perhaps the past will spill like a genie from this long-stemmed neck and delicate lip.

Alexis shouts and lobs rocks at a bobbing water bottle, gashing its plastic belly so it folds beneath a wave and sinks through a world suspended—blue cool dream where clear plastic bags slip like jellyfish. Perhaps in a hundred years a boy will dive here and pick through food tins bearded with seaweed, empty as hunger. When he shoots to the surface, his fingers will grasp the neck of what used to be our water bottle. Will he open it hoping to find a note inside, or does he take the bottle as the message? He'll wipe it off, guess the brand name, then toss the bottle back, bad catch, into the ocean of discarded things.

What good is it to make these stories up? The bottle rolls on the ocean floor or slips into a fisher's net with a catch of tuna. And I still come back to this urn, pocked with the dried body cavities of molluscs whose names I could never guess: limpet, sea butterfly, nudibranch, chiton. Dead now. Scoured with salt and sun, their white bone ears hear nothing. Their thousand mouths are open.

Karavi Beach, Serifos, Greece

42

Parable of Breughel's "Tower of Babel"

"Look at this painting," she said, and they were so happy they couldn't let it go, and as a game tried to recall all the small events that led them here: the slow afternoon reading in filtered forest light, the calm dinner talk, how she ran her fork across the tines of fish spine, trying to make a tiny music; and though the whole of it made only a shifting sort of sense, nothing built or proven, she said, "It is like climbing a latticework of sentences to the pinnacle of the word I am speaking now."

But what happens loses presence, like the owl that dives outside the window screen then settles on a ghost branch inside their heads, and so he finds himself past midnight working at his desk while she sleeps alone. Yes, he wants to be in bed with her, so they can clamber up each other, hand by hand, but an urgency keeps him fighting sleep until the window whitens, as if his pen could take him back to the moment she looked up from her book, smiling, and said, "Come on, sweetheart, you have to look at this."

Look at this painting where on toothpick ladders workers crawl high up the stepped structure into the crown of scaffolding, with teeny boards and hammers, buckets of plaster, trying to patch up the broken world and imagining a heaven to climb toward as the great plates belowground begin to shift. And look at the top edge of the painting, where no shining ladder punctures the clouds, yet with enough hope to split your heart a worker seeks one more rung, stretching a toy hand into sky.

That would have been a good place for the poem to end, back when he was in love and twenty-five, but look at him, age forty-five, still trying to get back to that night by adding lines that take him further off. He could write down the way she kissed him awake that morning, how much in love they thought they were, the day she sat next to him on the couch, laid a hand on his knee and told him that she couldn't anymore. He could, but that's another poem and this one is built on nothing, tumbling fast. Look quick, before it's gone.

Parable of the Found Objects (Pablo Picasso, 1945)

Do you remember the bull's head I made
from objects found discarded, handle bars,
a bicycle's old leather seat, spare parts
I welded into one and then displayed
at an exhibit? Then the critics said,
"Look how cleverly he formed it, how
he made the horns, look at the leather snout.
It's beautifully rendered, this bull's head."
I made those objects new. But now I say
the metamorphosis will be complete
when the sculpture is cast on a trash heap
with other fallen objects, and some day
someone takes them home because they're just right
as handle bars and seat to fix his bike.

Parable of the Translator

In the spirit of scientific inquiry, a surgeon tried to step outside of his own skin so he could see what skin was. First he carefully applied a scalpel to himself, and then shucked the skin off like a wetsuit. There it was, draped on the chair, like a deflated blow-up doll, and there was the surgeon, all raw nerves, staring at his punctured self and screaming. Quickly, he stepped back into his skin, and stitched himself up again, but now his fingers were on his feet, his toes were on his hands, his mouth spoke from between his buttock cheeks, and his long white beard hung down from his crotch. His wife ran in and yelled, "My God! What have you done with yourself?" But the scientist just pursed his buttocks into a smile and said calmly, "I've made myself into something entirely new." "But your skin," she wept, "What have you done to your skin?" "Oh, sweetheart," he said, kindly, caressing her cheek with his horny toes, "Why do you have to be so literal?"

Parable in Praise of Violence

"Violence is as American as cherry pie."
—H. Rap Brown, former Black Panther justice minister

Thanks for the violence. Thanks for Walt's rude muscle
pushing through the grass, for tiny Gulliver crushed
between the giant's breasts. Thanks for Moby's triangular hump
and Ahab's castrated leg. Thanks for the harpoons.
Thanks for this PBS history of the automatic pistol.

The good machine is simple, few moving parts,
an efficiency of what's preserved and what is wasted,
so with each shot the recoil cocks the gun to shoot again,
then recoil, cock and shoot again, recoil, cock,
and so on till the target buys it, or your ammo's spent.

Thanks for the poem, which is really a little pistol:
load and cock, point and aim, then the trigger,
the hammer, the powder, the discharge, the bullet,
the target, the recoil, the crime. No smoking gun,
just ballistics, caliber, powder marks, the question *why*.

My life is like a loaded gun, and when I aim it at you
I hope to take off the top of your head,
no safety on, no playing nice, just the spark,
the flash, the damage, just red American
cherry pie violence. So, thank you

for the harpoon gun we aim at God and death
and all the unknown world, and for the spear-stuck beast,
rope ripping through torn hands, for what
refuses to be caught and what we fathom only by
riding the whale down into the deep, refusing to let go.

Parable of the Desultory Slut

When he read in the obituary section that he was dead, the famous author was at first amused and flattered. *They love me so much,* he thought, *they have imagined me dead because they fear the loss of my genius above all else.* So he put on his hat, combed his goatee to a waxed point, and sauntered out of his flat to attend his own funeral. *How literary,* he thought, *like Huck Finn,* and *Everyone will be weeping.*

He was perturbed, however, when he found that the funeral home was in a bad section of town, next to a tattoo parlor named *The Desultory Slut.* He walked in past the unmanned front desk, to a back room of frayed velvet and gilt columns, where his coffin was on display, a faux mahogany monstrosity with painted pewter handles. The only people in attendance were four young professors from the local college, with leather patches on the elbows of their ill-fitting tweed jackets and long cruel faces of foxes and rats. He recognized one of them, a gangly fellow with pimply cheeks who had shaken his hand after his last reading and reverently asked for his signature.

Do you have one of my books to sign? the author had asked.

Oh, no, the young professor had cried, baring his hairless chest, *can you please sign here?*

Now the pimply fellow was sitting in a pew, whispering loudly to his neighbor, *Isn't it great,* he said, *The old bastard finally kicked.*

His neighbor nodded silently.

Deeply disturbed, but well aware of the dramatic potential of the moment, the author took this as his cue to step boldly into the room, with a loud *Ta daaa!*

For some reason, the professors ignored him, and continued their whispering.

For a moment, he was afflicted with a strange vertigo, and stood like a clay golem, without a will of his own. Then a sudden rage took him, and the author snapped out of the spell and strode to the front of the room, waving his arms. *Wait, I'm not dead at all. Here I am. It was all a mistake,* he cried.

But the professors did not see him. In fact one walked right through him, as if he were merely a ghost or spirit, and rushed up to the coffin. *Do you realize what this means?* the professor cried, *This means we're free,* and he grabbed the body in the coffin and dragged it to the floor. The shocked author saw in the body his own likeness, lips and cheeks rouged into a grotesque semblance of life.

He's dead, he's dead. Our enemy is finally dead, they chanted in a frenzy and the professors began trampling on the corpse, weeping with joy and relief.

Parable of the Ghost

The man who managed the rows of identical copying machines at the photocopy store took special care of his customers, priding himself that they could count on copies that would seem the same even under the unsparing eye of an electron microscope. The store itself was a franchise store of a chain that had metastasized in mini-malls across the States and western countries, with the same decor, the same machines, the same internal layout, and the same customer service script from the mini-mall in Ayacucho in the jungles of Venezuela by the Orinoco River to the great Italian-village-style outdoor walking mall of Fashion Island in Newport Beach, California.

When in a performance review his supervisors found out that he had deviated from the script, working with each customer for hours if necessary and using reams of extra paper and toner in search of the perfect copy, he was summarily fired. But as manager, he had the keys to the place, and for some months he had been living surreptitiously in the storeroom, sponge-bathing himself in the bathroom sink, eating sandwiches and sodas from the mini-fridge in the concession area. Now, instead of moving out, he padlocked the door from the inside, drew the blinds shut, and set out on the great experiment he had been cooking up in his lonely nights beneath the storeroom's hanging bare bulb.

He linked all of the machines together into one, copiers, fax machines, computers, and walked into the passport photo booth, drawing the curtain behind him like a customer at an XXX peep show, like a citizen entering a voting booth, like the wizard in a children's book. Instantly, the machines began to copy him, generation after generation of copies, copies upon copies, versions of him ghosting through the wires and circuitry with a whir and a spark and the acrid smell of burnt flesh.

When the police broke in some days later, he was gone, but now his phantom image began to appear like a watermark in the paper of copy machines throughout the chain. The customers complained, of course, about the bearded figure who stared at them from reproductions of their tax forms and divorce papers like a wild Rasputin, but nothing could be done. He had become the flaw in the glass distorting the light, the recessive gene subverting the chromosome.

Parable of the Footnote

There are those who trace the origin of the footnote to the graffiti carved in stone by Greek and Roman soldiers at the feet of the great colossi of Abu Simbel. Others trace it back to the characters painted on the toenails of the courtesans who served the corrupt courtiers of the Chen Dynasty, characters for peony flower and turtle head, silver stream and jade stalk, and of course characters for the mystical life-force at the heart of the world, the yin-yang essence that in the moment of climax becomes *jing*, the energy that will allow an ordinary man to become immortal. Still other scholars say that the origin of the footnote is the great lost Aramaic testament that is known only through the much redacted and distorted Greek of the New Testament. Like the work of the Gnostic heretics, it was known only through a scattering of references by scholars, the original having been ground underfoot by the sandaled heel of time.

Whatever its true origin, the footnote has ambitions to be more than it is in its late, fallen state, to restore itself to its perhaps mythical origins as a whole text from which it is a splinter, to be Prince Hamlet, not merely a courtier fit to swell a progress, not merely a pair of claws scrabbling through forgotten seas. But there are those who oppose such an idea, for without the foot, what will support the leg, and without the leg, the hip will fall, and without the hip nothing upholds the center of procreation, the belly and intestines through which the world makes progress, the arms that fight and the hands that caress the delicate cavity at the base of the spine while the lips make their safari across the lover's neck and chest. What good the broad back of an Atlas, strong enough to shoulder the world, if he teeters on footless stumps? "Upon the progress from foot to head, all things depend. From this order, comes the order of the cosmos," says Confucius in a little-known analect. "The footnote is the keystone without which the building will collapse," writes Da Vinci in coded reverse script written in his secret journals. The Masonic mysteries themselves are a code in which the levels of the order reveal secret upon secret, each built upon the one below. Without the first level, there can be no higher mystery.

None of this is a comfort to the poor footnote, who remains crushed under the weight of blocks of text, spat upon and ignored like the homeless that line the streets of our great metropolis. It curls there upon its dirty sleeping bag, ranting and shaking its green bottle. The forgotten history of the footnote is itself a footnote to history, abandoned like the footprints of those who walk on and don't look back. And the fate of the footnote is surprisingly widespread. In the realm of the scholars, literature has become a mere note to the theory and criticism invented to explicate it. In the parlors of Berkeley, the wild-eyed anarchists and communists still dream of red revolution while the people of China and Russia perm their hair and launch start-up dot-coms. The magi and messiahs who competed with Jesus to save the world, who thrilled the populace of Jerusalem with the magic of flight, with lightning drawn from the sky, with conversions of sheep to dog, all the Simons and the Elymases, are lost in the dust of libraries. The footnote cruises Internet dating sites, gazes in pornographic awe at the gifs and JPEGs of women who are looking for a man taller than him, and dreams of a lover who would trample his naked body with her beautiful feet. The footnote ducks when he hears loud sounds, suffers the indignities of proliferating dings in his car's paint job, the slings and arrows aimed at him by his boss, the airlines that charge him for two seats to accommodate his depressed and considerable girth. Yet his dreams are the dreams of the peasant who becomes the Emperor and founds a dynasty of blood and luxury, he is the worm that turns into something worse, the steel spikes that puncture the tires of the Mercedes, and on his flag is the snake coiled around a leg, fangs buried in the crotch, the bear trap in which is caught the paw of the lion rampant, and the words, almost unnoticed, inscribed in small black letters across the bottom:

Don't tread on me.

Parable of the Hunter

There is an animal that is marvelous because it doesn't exist. Like the unicorn, when you look at it closely, it turns out to be a two-horned oryx seen from the side, or a deformed goat. And yet in the moonlight . . . . Medieval allegorists have figured the creature in their Bestiaries as a symbol of the poet's recalcitrant inspiration or of evasive love, though modern critics have understood it as a manifestation of those elusive forms that fall between categories, such as the prose poem.

Although its meat is considered of dubious value, this is a product of ignorance. Those who know will go to almost any length to obtain it. The hunter of this beast will spend weeks in the forest listening to the trees until he has achieved the necessary silence, then will stand very still, his breaths as shallow as a Los Angeles conscience, waiting for the beast, and turning green. Centuries pass. The cities crumble like bread into the seas. The beast still has not come. By now, the hunter is half buried in the forest floor. He peers out from a tangle of strangling vines, covered with forest grubs, his long hair rooted in the earth.

For the first century, his thoughts had been rapid and filled with regret. *Why am I such a fool? Even if I capture the thing, no one will care. They like the caged creatures at the zoo, with their well-studied habits and habitats, with children poking them through the bars and mustached janitors to clean up their feces. Even if I could capture it, the biologists won't know what to call it, and so they'll call me a fraud. And what of Mary? I told her I would be back in a week.*

In the second century, his thoughts became a slow cycling like the sap inside the trees. Warmed by the sun, they would rise, driven by some hidden hydraulic pressure, and in the coolness of night they would subside and harden into a thick dreaming. In the third century, his face is cracked and brown as tree bark, and his thoughts have stilled and almost stopped, but on certain nights, as tiny full moons reflect in the dark marbles of his eyes, a great unspoken word ripples out as if from the ground and the trees themselves. It says, *come!* That's all, but each month it grows louder in its silence: *come!* COME! *COME!* The beast still does not come. And slow tears well from the hunter's eyes, crusting his cheeks with salt.

In another century, the hunter is dead. And, now that he no longer exists, the creature appears. It steps out from a fold in the air, like an actor from a stage curtain, and on long, silver legs delicately approaches the hunter's corpse. It parts the vines and hair with its slender nose, and licks the crusted salt from the hunter's cheeks. It is so beautiful, but who is left to see it? Only the great-great-great-great-great-great grandson of the hunter, who has wandered off from the camp-ground and gotten lost in the deep woods. He stares at the great animal with its tufts of hair like frosted wind, its wild dark eyes, its form shifting and slipping in the mind, neither this nor that. He puts out his tiny hand, and in a cracked, trembling voice calls out, *Come here, puppy. Here, pup!*

Parable of the Unwritten

The story was almost ready to spring full-grown from his head, like an ancient Greek god clothed in armor and wisdom, spear in her hand. This was the story he thought of while returning from the musty party, driving Whittier Boulevard past used cars for sale at Hadidy's, *0% Down! Su Trabajo Es Su Credito!* past the diner and the tatty motel, and he sketched it out in his mind, building up the parts like an anatomical drawing, the skeleton that would support it, the muscu-lature that would move it, the tendons that would connect it, the skin that would give it style and peel back at the dramatic moment to reveal the death's head inside, grinning its old joke. Soon he would be home, hurdling the cat in the doorway and scurrying to his office chair in a frenzy to type it up before the elements disappeared, leaving him just a face with no nose, a four-fingered hand.

But on Hadley Street he saw the sign for the YMCA approaching and on an impulse turned into the parking lot. Last night he'd had dinner at the apartment of a woman much younger than him and they'd talked and talked until two in the morning, but when he'd asked her, *Karen, are we on a date?* She'd replied, *I think we're just hanging out.* And so he fled into the gym. The gym smelled strangely of skunk and sweat, and the muscle-swollen beefcakes who were there at nine o'clock on a Friday night bad-eyed him, this middle-aged man reeking of cheap, professorial wine, wearing his brown Mexican leather sports jacket, dress shoes, and his black dress shirt embroidered in red with the Chinese character for *Dragon*. But he battered the weights for a good hour, until the scar tissue in his shoulders flamed like fiery filaments and the endorphins surfaced and sported in his brain like finned dolphins, because a body at rest is a body that's dead.

When he walked out again, the story had evaporated into the night sky. It was gone so completely it was as if it had never existed, and yet in his mind he still sensed the air it would have displaced had it gathered its limbs together and walked out into the world. He rushed home and dog-eyed the blank computer screen, as if the words might rise there like thin green tendrils sprouting in a field after the rain. But no. The blank screen said just variations on its one good word: blank, blonde, bland, blanch. It was the deleted sentence, the unknowing and the undreaming, the snow plain become the Zen master's mind, the whiteness of the whale disappearing into the deep, the void that stares back but which says nothing. And though he sensed it submerged in the margins of the page, in the tab and the space bar, the story never returned. He never wrote the story, and Karen never did more than hang out with him, and the fiery filaments in his shoulders only got worse. This was the story of his life, unwriting him, all of his worried charm, wrinkled beauty, unsaid brilliance. It unwrote him a little more each day, pulling back the skin of the world and revealing that old joke whenever he rested in bed, staring at the ceiling and fighting sleep, or went Twilight Zone on the couch. The rest is silence.

The California Book of the Dead

Gospel of the Golem of Los Angeles

The students glisten with youth. Every one of them is beautiful.
The world has yet to enter them and breathe away their souls.
I want to be like the children, but I am dirt and clay.
I woke one day and told myself, Stand up and walk like a man!
I raised my dust up out of bed and looked into the mirror
but couldn't read the word written by my forehead lines.
I keep a piece of paper under my tongue and on it one word: be.
So I write my way into my life, trying to name it as it leaves
and walk this clay around, a thing empty of belief.
My body's covered with hair, just like a human being,
but my hands are sticks; my brain's in rags. These days
I feel the hand of death on my forehead and it feels like a relief.

Parable of Houdini's Last Show

Once upon a time there was a magician
who climbed into his hat and disappeared.
It must have been a relief from all those years
of mastering the shitting doves and fickle rabbits,
the mirrors and boxes and assistant with sequined breasts,
to give himself away completely, the way he used to do
with the lover who parted for him like the sea,
and gripped the short hairs at the back of his neck,
whispering, "Come now, come inside me."
He's good at that, pouring himself away
like orange juice into a glass and then crushing
the carton and tossing it into the garbage.

He throws knives at his assistant,
cuts her in half and *poof!* makes her disappear,
but he doesn't really have the heart for this work.
He steps outside and asks himself, why
does everything have to be loss and loss?
See the stars burning off in the blackness above,
just pissing away their energy for forever
and a day and then they're dead?
Sometimes he wishes the Bomb would just go off
and turn everything into white light,
the theater whirling into sky, and all you
in the audience yielding all your atoms at once.

Harry has given it all away and left nothing.
That's his magic act. Why bother to fix the deck?
His life has been shuffled into other lives

until he can't tell what voice is speaking,
and from what stage, or why he's standing
in the kitchen crying, or why he saws himself
to pieces and moans himself awake at night,
why he blows up in a puff of confetti and rains
down to earth like the sorrow of the gods.
He called up his friend to tell him he was turning
forty, and "Look, Harry," his friend laughed,
"it's easier if you don't think of yourself
as half dead. Think of yourself as half alive."
And who can tell how he lived ever after?

The Californian Book of the Dead

I'm scared, so I'm writing this book of the dead,
a last testament, like James Kidd, Arizona prospector
mining the edge of Superstition Wilderness,
maybe murdered in Haunted Canyon for his gold,
whose will left his half million to research the spirit
because "I think in time we will photograph the soul
leaving the human at death." Perhaps we will, or perhaps
there's no will left when the body, sleeplike, settles
and the mind breaches, and the last neurons flaring in a final
visionary chain try to understand the storm wind ripping us
from our bodies, the million tiny Buddhas crawling down
the eyelids, white buddhas, red buddhas, blue and yellow.
The teenager daydreams super powers, walking invisible
into the girls' locker room and bank vaults, a super punch
that sends the football jocks sprawling, but doesn't dream
of the body's simplest power—the power to stop.
The body has its own will, and so I leave this testament.

Crack wide the doors of the sky, let my spirit leap
into heaven like a grasshopper, let me float among the stars
and eat the gods, and when I stand before the lords of death
I'll testify that I leapt from the pit of dreams each morning
and tried to live my life awake, that I gave twenty dollars
to the woman by the freeway entrance with the *Homeless
and Humiliated* sign while the red truck honked behind me,
that I bowed my head and dug with my tongue
between my lover's legs, that I mined that cave
and the gold for me was the pleasure she felt, but I did not
sleep with that woman at the French bistro who was so bored

of her husband and her little girls. I lived the best I could.
And if the mind breaks down in death, and the last neuron
fires in darkness like a sun snuffed out in a dying galaxy,
and if I wander for a while alone and find no god,
no rat, no earthworm, no butterfly of the spirit realm,
then let this be my superpower, the ability to speak
without breath, to write without fingers, to streak like
a meteorite across a black screen, and to go on and on
without will or consciousness, just these dead words
dancing before your eyes, a toy skeleton on a string.

Parable of the South Pole Buddha

" . . . the most tiny quantity of reality
ever imagined by a human being"

A physicist is stuck in a bunker at the South Pole,
freezing his burrito off, and trying to detect the rare light
given off by one in six billion neutrinos streaking through
the glacial ice, and it turns out he's a guy I like
talking poetry with sometimes and before he zooms
to the white continent he tries to explain neutrinos to me,
like a priest describing the progress of the spirit to a child.

No, they're not that three-piece punk band
from Philadelphia, making dancers oscillate in clubs
then fall into each other like so much dark matter.
Like most of us, they have a mean life and a half-life.
Like most of us they decay too fast. But here's the wonder:
these particles are so tiny, so unaffected, they shoot
right through the planet and through us without so much
as setting an electron quivering like a dragonfly's wing.

I wish I could do that, instead of lying in bed,
feeling gravity glue me to the indentation in the mattress,
wish I could jet right through the world
like cosmic rain, a flight of neutrinos shaped like a poet
and riding on the magic carpet of a weightless bed.
No tax forms, no lawyers, no dentists to drill
through the crown to the rot and murder the root—
just stick my face in the pillow and jellyfish through.

I try to let go of my body, to drop without a parachute,
a little Buddha, neither hot nor cold, but I can't lift off
like my friend who's gone to glacial nowhere
and who sets up his machines while the unseen wind
whishes by into the heart of cold, thinking
he can measure the invisible, thinking he might actually
understand what distinguishes us from nothing.

Parable of the Arrow

"An arrow of false ideas, smeared with love-poison,

has pierced your heart, yet you do not wish to pull it out.

So you cast yourself into darkness."

—Nagarjuna's *Treatise on the Great Perfection of Wisdom*

Here's what happens: one day an arrow sails
from the sky, plants itself right in your chest.
You cry out, grab it with one hand. But if
you pull it out, you die. The Buddha says
to let go further, let go faster—death
just seems disastrous. Buddha says to give
up lust, pull out that shaft—it's worse to burn
than fade away. He says to live in time
is fruitless. Buddha is so full of it.

You are alive because you feel death worm
into your chest, so though you're bleeding wine,
you have your jackets tailored till they fit
around the arrow. Turning in your bed
or making love, the arrow pricks the worst.
It burrows deeper, but you live with it.
You lay your hand against your punctured chest
and pledge allegiance to the hurt. It's worth
the pain to know (just maybe) you exist.

Terminal Testament

Please answer quickly, without taking time to think. What is your destination? How much time have you spent on earth? Did you speak to the panhandler who stands outside the terminal? Did he kiss you? What did he tell you was wrong with you? Did he give you anything to hold—his heart, his sweat, his diseases?

What is the total value of all the goods you have given away in your lifetime? What is the total amount of hours you have been asleep? Look straight ahead and open your eyes. Why do you look so surprised? Please stand against the wall, behind the red painted line. Please stop shouting.

Has anyone given you any dreams to carry for them or did you pack them away yourself? Are you carrying more than ten thousand miles of memory or oblivion? What have you signed your name to? Please stand up and face the front. Please wait patiently. Please, I just work here. I don't enjoy this. Please, I can't stand it when you shout.

Spell for Balancing Stones

"And some are loaves and some so nearly balls
We have to use a spell to make them balance"
—Robert Frost, "Mending Wall"

The bearded sculptor kneels in sand and lifts
a sea-smoothed loaf of granite in both hands like a baby.
Head bowed, eyes closed, listening to a silence inside,
he lightly sets the rock atop a small globe teetering atop
a spine of sea-stones swayed to one side like a hula dancer.

Behind him each wave comes to shore and applauds.
Buddhists say waves are thoughts breathing into mind
and retreating. They're all we know of the world.
Yet past them is an ocean to drown in, and by the ocean
runs the highway out of town into mountain rainforest.

In this jungle past the guardhouse on the cliff top
is a dream house with a wet bar, walls painted with murals
of feathers and stars, blossoms and jaguars, with lounge chairs
by the pool where the millionaire settles now with cocktail
and young wife to watch the sun alight

on the horizon, dyeing the sky tequila sunset.
And though everything is stacked so high its own weight
pulls it down, and though the forest ceiling leaning overhead
constricts like a green throat, he listens to the Pacific lick
its tongue below and imagines ways to stop the world's heart

from beating his heart away, to hold the equilibrium between
two waves, the way, in the stone garden back in town,
the sculptor kneels among piles in frail balance, still holding
the final rock at the top, and a hush runs electric through
the crowd in loud sunhats as he shifts grip, leaning in to feel

the tiny impulses to fall forward, fall back, but always to fall.
The ocean sucks in a breath. In Buddha's open palm
the billion universes arc and threaten to crash.
The sculptor raises his head and, eyes still closed,
lightly he lifts his hands away from the stone.

Promenade, Puerta Vallarta, Mexico

Parable of the Mummified Cat

The cat who lived in the wine cellar we'd converted
into a spare bedroom had torn through the screen and leapt
to the rim of the ancient urn below the high window
then down to the lip of the old stone oven and from there lightly
to the floor. It must have made our summer home
its wintering den to escape the cold rain and the villagers
with poison and sticks. But when I forced open the stuck door
and stepped in I saw just dust and webs and thousands of black rat
turds and the clay urn overturned and broken into two jagged pieces—
it must have teetered and crashed as the cat leapt off,
so the cat was trapped inside the dark stone room
and that's where I found it, behind the mattress tilted against a chair
so as not to mildew, curled into the mosquito net, so long dead
and mummified the waterless body had flattened into a relief
of a cat, just hair tufting off dried flesh and fanged skull.
The rat turds, swept up, turned out to be the husks
of wall grubs, who must have feasted on the corpse in thousands
and been in turn caught and webbed and poisoned
and slung and drained by the hanging spiders.
And for a while in the dark where the cat clawed light fixtures
out of the wall and screamed and mewed and curled up at last
to dream its last life off there was a kind of order here,
though not a kind order, and there were great feasts all through
the dank black winter until I came with broom and detergent
and sunlight and nudged the corpse into a plastic bag
with the broom handle and killed the spiders and swept up
the bug husks and scrubbed at the dark cat-shaped stain
on the floor until everything came off except a black
impression of the tail. And I had electricity and mops.

And in the wine cellar where the cat had lived I put the music on
extra loud and tried to put what happened out of mind.
And the stench flew out the windows. And I soaked the net in bleach.
And I washed my hands three times. And I put everything
back into order, the kind of order I could live with.

The Suckee, Fuckee, Blowjob Sutra

Suckee, fuckee, blowjob? call the prostitutes
from the mouths of shabby shacks,
and I am fourteen and now my uncle Jack is offering
a woman ten bucks, five bucks, to do my brother
and me together, trying to make us squirm.

And now I am forty-five, typing black words
across a bright screen in the five a.m. dark,
because night presses the window with so much erotic promise
and something that feels important has been eluding me
and the face that peers out of the dark window at me
is the face of an old man I don't recognize.

And now I'm twenty-five and I walk downstairs
into the cavelike dark of a Berkeley pizzeria
where the line of video games chants come-ons
like hopeful wallflowers at a teenage dance,
with mirror-ball lights in their eyes.

And when I'm in the game I'm the kick-ass king,
the one-armed warrior of the wasteland, Jean-Paul Sartre
with a strap-on shotgun, blasting my way
across the No Exit stage, jiggling myself towards
the climax that comes when the pattern comes clear.

But beyond the pattern is another pattern,
beyond each level is another level, and I've lost
quarters, faith, and patience and so I turn
from the machine and sprint into the numinous
white rectangle at the top of the stairs.

And yes, I'm overeducated, so it reminds me
of the Parable of the Cave when I leap like Nijinsky
through glass doors into *to kalon*, into the *mysterium tremendum*,
or at least into the pastel light of California,
leaving the basement level and reentering the world

of messages gabbling on the far side of sense:
digital phones diddling with satellites, mouths
and tongues playing the wind instrument of the throat,
streetlight grammar conjugating traffic,
panhandlers panhandling, handbills posted
so thick the telephone poles have inch-fat paper vests,

and all of it so hopeful, and all of it calling *suckee,*
calling *fuckee,* calling *blowjob,* though I censor it out.
And yet, just now, when I look down at my feet
one message spray-painted on the concrete slips through:
"Who really needs a red wheelbarrow?"

And, as my mind wheels that question back and forth,
trying to decide if it's empty or a load,
an open Jeep yowls up, loaded with whooping frat boys
in baseball caps and wife-beaters, and one pumps his fist
and in perfect Californese shouts to me
and no one else in the world, *Carpe diem, Dude!*

Spell Against Disease

White milk of the body, the body's stiff cream.
See the potato of the body, just a thin tan skin
over the creamy blank of the flesh.
If you cut off an arm, the chalk moon of the stump
will not bleed. It will shine like a statue, inert
and solid as hard taffy or porcelain or marble maybe.

White milk of the body, the mind's white hive.
Like jointed plastic dolls we lift soup to our lips
and salsa dance and drive our cars
and never bubble up from the yellow heat
of infection, never grow a crop of polyps
and goiters, free radicals and tumors.

Sweet milk, sweet cream, and everything inside is clean
and sanitary like bathtubs or plastic cutting blocks,
and our blanched lips part in a smile
to show the snowy teeth and the pink shock
of tongue serpenting inside.

The sun is bleaching us to bone and we are children
sifting the stones and cracks in our pants.
We make love on the ghostly beach,
the desert planet of the sheets,
and nothing squeezes from the white leather breasts,
from the pallid worm, and nothing lives inside us
but white milk of the body, the body's hard cheese.

The Nihilist Sermons

The Dead God Codex

Who knows what the world is? I charged
my Nietzsche textbook at the bookstore,
hoping that some grandeur after the death of God
would flame out shining from the pages,
but I was shaken, crushed like foil, the shopboy
scowled at me, damn him and his nose ring,
the cumulonimbus clouds gathered greatness,
dark, like the ooze of oil, and I ran among crushed men
reckoning how far to my car as the fat drops
fell like rods, generating splashes as I trod,
and all the neons seared my eyes, trading words with me,
Vacancy, Tattoos, Hot Croissants, as through the bleared
smeared window of the French Bakery the female baker
toiled wearing a man's smudged shirt and shared
with this man the smells if not the flesh, if not the soil
or soul, no bare foot feel of being in the shoddy world,
no croissant for me.

Nature is somewhere, spent but there, and still,
one guesses, living, since that's what nature does,
living with the dear freshness of deep things,
but I lived then in Los Angeles, and, home,
looking out the window as the last lights
blackened to the West, I went traveling towards morning,
riding my soggy bed, until from the brown smoggy brink
of the world eastward came springing what
we have instead of the Holy Ghost, bent sunlight
over the world brooding, warm, comforting
as breasts, flying on one bright wing.

The Sermon on Los Angeles

1. *Coming in to Los Angeles*

Like silver balls in a pinball machine,
the traffic ricochets from lane to lane
and red nerves weave across the painted lines
as drivers honk and blare and curse and scream
inside their little spaceships. In her bubble,
one car over, a woman flashes brights
like bared teeth at a cruiser without lights
but the gang bangers in the car are trouble:
the boys fall into orbit next to her,
shouting *You bitch! You cunt!* The driver leans
precariously out the window, lines
her up in his sights, calls out *"Look here, whore!"*
and shoots with thumb and finger, laughs and drives
on, arms tattooed with stars and tits and knives.

2. *In Simi Valley*

I smell the slaughterhouses and the ovens,
fantasies cooked until they fall from bone.
Here everyone is *uber* hip, the covens
of Wiccans worshiping the goddess on
the cell phone, tinkling gold and opening
their word holes. Dad plays pool in his new den
and won't say much. A flat screen boob tube sings
to a room empty as a mind gone Zen.
And here the popeyed daughter pads her bust,
the teenage boy gets zonked with a towel rolled

and wet by the door crack. Their every dream
has been pre-dreamed and tested, until just
the smallest feelings rattle, rattle-boned
like plastic skulls attached to a key ring.

3. *Azusa Boulevard*

I'm driving out the boulevard past icons,
orange planets floating over the gas
stations, the Tiki-Tiki Lounge, the iron
sky, the convenience store where (for a pack
of cigarettes, eleven dollars and
a hat) the Pakistani clerk was shot
last week, the city like a void expand-
ing through the towns of lemonade, the lot
of polished marked-down cars below the free-
way, dark smog pushed against the hills, a fat
man to the table, galaxies of dust,
the low sky stained with nicotine and rust.
Los Angeles. A billboard explains that
Life Is Harsh. Your Tequila Shouldn't Be.

The Sermon on Being a Man

1. On Being a Man

If at the party I am the one lying on the floor
and throwing grapes at women,
going ape shit and hoping to make the beast
with two backs,

if men are a hybrid of plants and ghosts,
doing the shoulder dance on the carpet,
despairing over their puddly bodies
and trying to shed their skin,

if soul is only a word leaving the body
like smoke from lipsticked lips
rising and dispersing out on the balcony,

then what?

2. Drinking at The Well

Cold as a witch's tit outside The Well.
Inside I sit against the cushioned wall
and watch the people drinking Burning Bushes,
Hot Kisses and Black Summers, with small dishes
of finger snacks to fill the hunger gap.
The dick-smack by the door is saying that
"She's got a serious badonkadonk
butt." "And a half," his friend agrees. They're drunk
and love's a bottle by an empty shotglass.

Sex is the stick that coats her lips with gloss.
But they're small men with movies reeling through
their brains, they're pimply perves who have bad shoes,
amped up on Lady Snow and full of lack,
and I can see they are ass out of luck.

3. *Visit to the Liquid Kitty*

Persuasive supple dancer blooming pretty
by the wet-bar with a nightshade sigh, you're
such a Chiquita banana, such a Betty.
Please, bust this losing streak, show me the door
to your red heart or your blue bed. It's true
I'm just a bonehead, but even hair-shirt-
ers with thorn-whips and stakes need sex. And who
can really grasp how strange it is to flirt,
how queer we are to strangers? I have seen
them smoking in the streets outside of clubs
and perving at each other. I have seen
the tilted pink neon cocktail glass, pubs
whose patrons think, *knock boots, suck face, muff dive,*
and *boff.* They're thinking with the trouser snake,
the pecker, peter, boner, pud. They live
to get retarded, get stupid. They ache
to get inside your body. Yes, I know
I'm one of them. My life is on the fritz.
I can't think my way out of this one, so
I'm thinking, *whoopie, nookie, quickie, jizz.*

The Sermon on Drugs

1. *Lecture on Illicit Drugs*

I lie down in the bed and feel as though
I am free falling or that time is flying
through me. I watch the room contort and flow
in strange geometries. Although I'm trying
to get up, gravity it seems is turned
to "high," and all my bones are golden. Now
my friends are permafried. Now they have burned
their brain cells out, they speak too fast or slow.
They corner you or sit themselves and rock
in corners at a party. They tell you
they've learned the road of excess leads to hope
or wisdom, something like that. What a crock.
It's just a spider thread that ties us to
the earth. I think we need a stronger rope.

2. *Remembering His College Daze*

Wake up bright youth with neurons granular
as eye goop cereal! Some way to start
the day, with acid indigestion, fart,
and stretch as I traverse the dorm to far
Men's Bathroom with its bluesy door, jet
through last night smells past passed-out and beer-breathing
and lounged-across-the-lounge-couch-stuttering-
snores-alta-forte-on-the-nose-trumpet
Mike, the half-dead football halfback, once busted
for dealing coke and two schools later here,

cleaned up, if somewhat alcoholic, beer
can smushed against his head, his face encrusted
with *ugh*. Not me. Unzip, watch Willie dangle,
an acrobat in air, my carnal angel.

3. *Lecture while Hiking in the Angeles Crest Wilderness*
   with a Group of College Students

What's the difference between a poet and a large pizza?
A large pizza can feed a family of three.
Ba-dum-dum!
Do I have your attention yet?

The fountains are louder at night.
It takes a mind of darkness to know them.
I think you need to learn to shush.

Students, you need some face time with your souls.

I heard you talking about me last night,
"The prof's about to shit a cold purple twinkie!"
Then you yorked out the vodka and Red Bull,
crashing through poison oak.
Students, today you got stoned in your tent,
then hiked through the wilderness singing
Disney songs and parsing the difference between
bodacious secretaries and nurses in tight white tops.

Students, eternity is bent.
The world is without meaning.
Do you know you will be crushed like a beer can?
The human fish wriggles and wriggles with happiness,
biting at a hidden hook.

The Sermon on the Poets

When in the chronicle of wasted time
I turn off MTV
and read another slender gorgeous book,
I think how weary I am of poets
with their blowsy beauties
with two lips like unto two cherries
and cushion-thumping about
deadly death among the *bare and ruined choirs.*

Futzing with words,
they try to caulk the cracks
in their philosophy with bumsquabble,
make little worlds up cunningly
of Derrida and angelic spit,
but they're unclean as Cupid's itch.
Like con artists they cloud their waters
to make them seem profound.

They write with the angels' amber voices.
They have to, because they stammer,
blurt out drippy tummy lines.
Peacock of peacocks,
with vanity *as wide as 'twere the sea*,
they're certain with the proper education
the rest of us
would give a fiddler's fuck.

The Sermon on God

1. *The Mirror Psalm*

I had a dinner with a woman mad
for God. I told her I have learned to walk
without a crutch. She told me I was made
to look like him but I have always thought
he has my nose. So am I God's worst blunder
or is he mine? She told me I should raise
my children in my image. That's bad taste,
it seems to me. She talked about surrender
and resignation, prudence, diligence,
but I preferred her company, her style
to his, the sweetness in her clear eyes. Still,
I might believe in God if he could dance,
a God who's learned to laugh, a God like this
young woman I press into for a kiss.

2. *What's Your Damage?*

God made a big noise in the world and then kicked off,
and since then we've been going medieval on each other.

A scientist replaces a cow's side with a plastic wall
so he can see its four stomachs digesting.
That's my metaphor for something.
Here we are in East Bumblefuck,
living if you can call it that at the spit-out butt-end of the universe,
and thinking we're God's gift. Of course we go bitchcakes
when we find we're not.

Everybody considers dying important, but big whup.
We're all smelling ripe. We should learn to die.
Sorry, no beer-goggles for this nihilist poet, let me munch out
on the green sweet grass. I don't want to be looking
when that nasty frat boy Death comes cow-tipping.

Look at these ants eating cat-droppings in the litter box.
Just try to be perfect as an animal.

3. *Riding the Crotch Rocket*

Sometimes the world will beat seven shades
of shit out of you before you brush your teeth,
but some days like today I am happy to be
kicking it in this janky universe,
riding my crotch rocket through the suburbs,
even though God or whatever
seems to be off somewhere dicking the dog.
Here's a thought, I'm coming to an intersection,
and sex and death are a perfect rhyme.
Here's a thought, a stop sign red as new blood,
and mister D is waiting to jump our bones.
Here's a thought, it's all too mondo bizarro,
the old gods lying buried beneath the sprinkler system,
the wheel of the sky revolving around the stargazer.
Here's a thought, I need love like a heart-attack
but I'm still jonesing for it. And the sign, after all,
says *Yield*.

Psalms of an American Childhood

1. *The Video Arcade Psalm*

When one boy's head is chopped off, he falls dead,
and bright blood squirts out from the lurid stump.
You fag, he says, *you got my fucking head.*
Give me another quarter, or I'll stomp
your face, he smiles. His soul leaves through the eyes'
movie projector, spills into the dream;
dark honey of his brain is crystallized
into men fighting on the video screen.
Then in the alley they chuck rocks until
black fur and wings seethe from the hive, but still
the wasps won't dive. They bumble like dumb bees
in midair. So the boys go home to play
"House of the Dead," though as the first boy says,
This game sucks dick. I'm sick of shooting zombies.

2. *The Tight Shoes Psalm*

Like too-tight shoes that irritate the toe,
a little red, a little raw, a bite,
some blood (you limp but still can't make it go
away with laces knotted double-tight),
this young boy scratches bites until they drip,
then scab, then irrigates until they run,
then grinds and picks with a steal steak knife tip,
since scars are cool and rushing blood is fun.
He excavates until it's permanent,
and burrows on and on and will not learn
despite the sober talks, the punishment

that grows. And when you feel the chafing burn
your skin, the grating scrape into your brain,
that's what he wants: to gash you with his pain.

3. *Psalm of Lucifer*

You open up your arms. The sky is vast;
it waits for you to spread your lemon wings.
Your father says you're going *nowhere, fast,*

but you're a schooner with each arm a mast,
your windbreaker the sail that whips and sings
against your open arms. The sky is vast

and—hair and dove wings flaming—you're the last
of Lucifer's flight crew, fighting all things
your father says. You're going nowhere, fast,

so run downhill and grasp the wind. The past
is death, but downhill are the wanderings
you open like your arms, like sky as vast

as gambling felt, as grass on which you're cast.
Your teacher says, *You all are queens and kings,*
but Father says you're going *nowhere, fast.*

Your shoulder's raw as watermelon, stings
where you hit dirt. Again you fan your wings
and open up your arms. The sky is vast.
Your father says you're going *nowhere, fast.*

Two Kenyan Parables

1. *Parable of Babu, the Dhow Captain of Lamu Island*

From loudspeakers the muezzin call out
the call to prayer, carried on cool wind,
the monsoon wind that blew in the devout
and the devourers, that helped them find
then found this island city where mangrove
and ivory and rhino horn and slaves
especially were traded. Quiet love
is in the eyes of Babu, who believes
in Allah and in fate. He speaks of how
one day his son falls from the steps and cracks
his skull and dies. Now Babu shifts the dhow
into the breeze, ties off the rope and tacks.
"We all are slaves to death," he says. "I have
three kids alive, all blowing toward the grave."

2. *Parable of Farid and the Elephants*

Farid stands at the stern end of the dhow
while Babu steers with one foot on the rudder.
He smiles and shouts, "Remember, Babu, how
when we were seven, elephants crossed over
from Manda Island?" "Yes," says Babu, rolls
a cigarette with one hand, lights it, smokes,
and shifts his foot and waits while Farid tells
the tale. "You should've seen how frightened folks
were then! They screamed and ran with heads turned back
and fell and broke a hand or crushed an arm

and then the elephants screamed back, and oh
they went insane, smashed boats. When they attack,
you have to shoot them dead. They cause such harm."
"And did you eat the beasts?" I ask. "No, no,"
Farid says, laughing. "We don't eat such meat.
Now hippo meat is good. Now that, I eat."

The Dating Sutra

1. In Which He Writes an Email to Joy

I heard that you were looking for me, Joy.
I'm here. Put out your hand and touch this screen
where pixels fizzle out like suns. The toy
heart in my chest will wind down, stop. I've seen
my death in the blank space that I embrace
at night, that loss. You're there. You understand
I'm lying. There's nothing there for my hand
but dreams of nothing solid, dreams of grace,
the way my stray cat, Shredder, kneads her claws
into my lap and dreams of nipples while
I type this poem. She's jealous of your smile
and tries to walk across the keys. Her paws
pick out some nonsense that I can't complete.
She's here. She's purring, walking towards "Delete."

2. In Which He Thinks of Her in the Web

I think I sense your ghost screened there
behind the pixels and each byte
of blue text, floating on null air
in ether just beyond my sight.
I think it would be easy to
drive you away with one wrong word
yet I send out each strand anew
like filaments from some absurd
spider who makes his patterns just
to catch the light, each filament

a string of words that someone must
receive beyond the world, each sent
like radio into the sky
to beat against the stars and die.

3. *In Which He Writes a Dating Sutra*

It's not the water we should know, that passes
through arteries and earth. It is the force
that through the green fuse drives the flower, source
of everything (even this man with glasses)
that we should know. It's not the salt that we
should know, but water where the bitterness
dissolves and all great matters matter less,
divorce and death and infidelity
and how the nervous man fidgets and twists
across the table. It's not salt that we
should know but flesh that salt preserves. We know
that flesh will rot and salt dissolve and wrists
turn watery, lose force, but why not be
in love till that day? Won't that do, for now?

4. *In Which He Muses on Saying No*

I'm trying not to love you but you fill
my breath and eyes, inflate my helpless brain
with blood and make me dream in luscious pain
awake. But *no*, I promised. I will kill
this lust for all of you, I'll try at least

to turn the switch off in my groin, reboot
my mind when it's locked up on you, to beat
my passions back into their cage like beasts,
try to say *no*. Let my brain not say *You,*
it's you I want. Just be responsible.
I'm trying hard but it's too hard a test
when everything inside me says to do
the opposite, to let myself grow full
of you, say yes to everything, say yes.

5. *In Which They Kiss on the Couch*

I see her pupils dilate like black ink
in soft white paper as her pelvis bone
bites into mine, and feel her spirit link
with mine, two bodies trying to be one
as she pours into me and holds my face
between her hands, and everything inside
me tells me I should be inside her, taste
her tongue and belly, flow in the deep tide,
but "No," she tells me, "Wait, we have to stop.
We will make love but we should do it right."
"I'm sensing that the time to wait is gone,"
I laugh, but no, she simply climbs on top,
breasts to my chest, long hair pouring blonde light,
and holds me gently, like a loaded gun.

6. *In Which He Goes to Hear Some Blue Jazz*

Perhaps I should stop writing poems to you
and just call up the deep-tissue masseuse
who grinned at me all through the show. And through
the set the singer smiled, sang jazzy blues
to me then later in the diner ran
her nails along my neck and leaned her cheek
against my biceps, purring, while her man
looked on. I leapt up asking for the check,
apologizing with my eyes. Perhaps
her music spellbound me, since when she stood
and leaned into my chest I almost lapsed
and kissed her. But I drove back home instead.
These days it seems all women are ablaze
with singing light. And they all have your face.

7. *In Which He Feels Aftereffects*

I'm reading at my desk, the afterword
of a new book, but cannot concentrate
because my mouth is filled with aftertaste
from an imagined kiss. And afterwards
I batter weights down at the gym, but after-
images hover in the mirror, floating dreams,
her green eyes watching me, the way she seems
to burst each time she detonates with laughter,
the way we stood too close that afternoon
at my place after lunch, and I moaned, "No,

it's hard to stop myself, you'd better go."
She hugged me fast and then she flew
to the door, laughing, while deep aftershocks
rang me and left me just these afterthoughts.

8. *In Which They Talk All Night on the Phone*

"Damn you," she laughs, "I can't get you out of
my mind." That's how I feel, out of my mind,
the way you might step out the door and find
yourself in a strange world, new stars above
spinning through emptiness without design,
attracted by some force no one can see.
Strange world, nice world, thank you for gravity
that pulls me into orbit 'round her mind
so that we speak all night like teenagers
across the darkness, linked by telephone
from head to head. She lies in bed alone,
listening to me pace, to my new verse,
and says, "I just can't sleep. My god, it's two,
we have to stop." "We do," I sigh, "damn you."

9. *In Which He Smells Her on His Fingers*

This is the scent persisting on my fingers.
This is the memory of soaping your
belly in the hot shower while your door
piled up with students. This is how it lingers
inside my pores, the smell of inside you.

This is the way I ran a nail along
the valley of your spine, took in my lungs
an inhalation of your hair—I drew
you towards me, drew a breath of you, allowed
myself to slip inside. This is the way
I kissed your eyelids, bit your lip, the day
that dawned while we were kissing on the couch,
the way you left, the way your scent remains.
This is the way I breathe you in again.

Sutra of Despair

1. *Concerning Putting a Gun to My Lover's Lover's Head*

I know a little bit about the gun
but never thought that I'd be thinking how
damn sweet I'd find it to be holding one
against the skull of one who holds you now.
A tape plays in my brain again, again:
he fucks you, he's on top and pins you down
so you can't move. That makes him come. And then,
to prove you don't own him, he turns around
and hits upon your young friend, twenty years
old, larger breasts than you. This is the man
for whom you gave me up. To stanch your fears
you tell him of my fantasy, or plan.
(To watch his head explode. That would be fine.)
He smiles and says, "Tell him to get in line."

2. *Concerning Ghosts*

You're ghosting. I am haunted. But the wire
fence rusting by the cemetery does
not symbolize our busted love. Red fire
that eats the metal is just rust.
Yet still you ghost through everything. A white mule shades
beneath a leaning tree, her large eyes gaze
at me (passing phenomenon that wades
the mountain grass with just two legs) and blaze
one question: Does that mean something to me?
No, she decides, and bends her head to eat.

Phenomena are empty; emptiness
is a phenomenon. The mule is free
to eat the simple grass. I eat defeat
and starve. Without you, ghost, this world means less.

3. *Concerning the Great Rift Valley*

And so I went to Africa. I was
running away from my heart. Forty-five,
alone again, but still a bit alive.
I came to Africa again because
I had no home at home. And so I drove
into the Rift, the great green valley where
the heart of Africa struggled to tear
itself in two, then calmed. Too much in love
to stay inside my life, I came to see
the great heart, strained and buckled but still whole
(though with a scar where salt lakes fizz, a hole
where yellow sulphur spits a magma sea).
I came ten thousand miles to gaze at it,
a heart that tore and strained but didn't split.

4. *Concerning Birding at Lake Baringo*

I watch as the goliath heron spreads
great wings and wades into the water, shut
the camera off after its shutter reads
the world, the bird, the lake, in focus—but
I have no clarity because you kept

your heart a secret, lied to me
for months and finally flew off and slept
with him. I watched the child and dog and he
climbed onto you. Inside the lens, I find
the world is coded with precision, things
are sunlit sharp. I watch. The heron flies.
But where's the clarity inside my mind?
My eyes confuse your smile, our years, dark wings.
I walk from room to room, believing lies.

5. *Concerning Malaria Dreams*

You're naked, sitting at the desk. I come
up from behind, caress your clavicle
and spread lotion on your breasts. Like some
white ghost you turn to me, kiss me with full
lips lip-sticked bright, bright red and gaze at me
the way you used to do, as if the most
amazing thing were in your sight. To be
that to you once again. That would be, ghost,
worth fever, sorrow, shakes, worth the disease.
It's just a needle prick, some small blood drained
and then it's in you, shivers, strange clear dreams
in which you look at me amused, at ease,
and nakedly in lust, in which you're pained
with joy and there's no cure (or so it seems).

6. *Concerning Homographs*

Last year I dropped off thirty pounds, content
to live my salad days on lettuce, raven-
ously unfilled, or unfulfilled, the content
of my poor heart a wish, a croaking raven
from someone else's poem, an unwound
dock line, a white-winged sailboat in the wind
that tacked out of my life. Now I'm a wound,
and you a *nevermore,* and nights unwind
towards dawn with dreams that scavenge like a dove
whose manic BB eye seeks through the refuse
for you. Today I ate some air then dove
back into bed alone. I won't refuse
the slightest anorexic hope. I close
my eyelash wings. No black bird brings you close.

7. *Concerning Terms*

A thinking person doesn't lightly state
"Her love is dead" when other words express
the medical condition. Understate:
say "moribund," or that "she loves you less."
"Cadaver" is the term for a cool corpse,
but don't say "The cadaver has been moved
to the morgue." Try to let the lover's hopes
down lightly; say "There's life till death is proved."
Then later, when the lover paces, crazing
the others in the waiting room, chest tight,

and hyperventilating, wild eyes gazing
at the white floor, "Her love expired last night"
is a good phrase. Now leave for your next call.
Try not to think all love is terminal.

8. *Concerning Self-Storage*

I packed up house, and set aside the fat
pants and the thin ones, shirts I'd never fill,
the books I'd never read and dishes that
I'd never use, and drove them to Goodwill.
More difficult were model cars, light sabers,
the books on how to raise a troubled child,
the knives we hid from him, his scribbled labors
at rock songs, toys he broke when he went wild.
Most troubling were the photographs of you
and me in Greece, the way you looked at me.
All stored away. Think of the good: it's true,
I've lost my family; at least I'm free.
But how can all that world fit in this box,
this coffin for our lives, this door, these locks?

9. *Concerning a Bath*

When you are very old and beautiful
and, soaking in the bath, look down upon
the slender form in which you lived, and full
with memory think of the lovers gone,
will you remember me in these last days,

a harried, weakened man, pathetic, lost
because there is no joy inside your gaze
when you see me? I broke before you tossed
me in the trash, it's true. Before the bath
turns cold, won't you recall me strong in loving
you, as a man made whole by you, forgiving
my faults? Please do. You loved me, then you stopped,
but we were great once. Great. Then pain, then wrath.
Oh, well. Remember me the way you must.

Five Philosophical Discourses

1. *Discourse on Love in the Ruins*

I sip a Nescafé and eavesdrop on
the couple next to me, the Asian teen
and milk-blonde girlfriend eating beets and greens.
Under the Athens sun, she is so blonde
you need smoked glass to see, her face so white
it bruises if you look at her, the slim
eyebrows disappearing into skin.
In a tan blouse she swells with light, is like
a laughing shifting cotton field. Breakfast.
I watch two flies dogfight against the sign,
watch a big man on a slow moped whine
by, his red-shirted gut quivering fast.
Against the sky the Acropolis—stained teeth
and fractured marble jawbone—also eats.

2. *Discourse on the Sunset as a Hermeneutic Cycle*

I'd like to capture how this gorgeous sun
turns all the world to gold, but since all things
have shadows, I can't help myself, I think
about the cancers sprouting un-
derneath the cute brown moles, dioxin in
the Belgian pork, the dogfish with its rows
of teeth, the man-of-war whose body glows
under the waves, its tendrils gelatine
like acid hair that scorches you on touch,
the stonefish with its poison spines. At last

I feel a vague pain simmer in my gut
like inspiration. But the dark comes fast
and I forget what quality I tried
to capture in this leaking brain and eyes.

3. *Discourse of Roses*

A world perhaps can fit inside a word,
a sword asleep inside its sheath, but no
thing can be created out of no-
thing and no word can sing outside the world.
A rose is not a rose is not a rose,
as it turns out because the rose turns in-
to something else, some blossoming red thing
at the mind's core, inverted, just a ruse
within the mirror, mirroring without
becoming, much less being. So how to be
when all things multiply their glassy poses
inside our eyes, confusing us about
the real and really false? The world we see
is just some word that fills our eyes (with roses).

4. *Discourse of the Poet to His Personae*

I made you up, and now it's up to you
to make me think that you exist. Inside
all things is gravity. Why do you hide
with it, like dark in shadows or like blue
in ice? What sort of thing is dead, a ghost,

but nonetheless thinks it invented me?
What loneliness, what dark necessity?
What makes a child design a man from snow
then look into the flat white face to see
if maybe in the charcoal eyes some hint
of being might ignite? What sort of word
from your ice mouth might tell me what to be?
What mystery chills underneath your hat?
What hunger makes me speak you like a world?

5. *Discourse on the Crippled God*

A man swings through the open doors on crutches,
his long arms thick with muscle like the Christ
whose marble shoulders shouldering the cross
are sculpted mighty as Odysseus'.
Before he crosses forehead, heart and chest,
the cripple leans one crutch against the wall
and dips his free hand in the carved stone well
of holy water. Hoping to be blessed,
he gazes at the painted ceiling, stays
a moment, hands crossed on a crutch, tame head
bowed. From the altar's speakers angels sing
while on one leg like a black stork, he prays,
his other pant leg pinned. If he's not dead,
God listens and as is his way does nothing.

Turtle Head Gospels

Gospel of Henry David Thoreau at the Circle K Convenience Store

Sure thing, Henry Thoreau, I'd like to live a life aware, but how
aware do I really want to be of time wrinkling and ripping my house,
town, corner store, my life with my wife together apart, chain
reaction exploding every moment until right now? As I walk
to the corner store, it seems beneath notice, like hidden insect
monarchies who rise feudally, Chinese mini-dynasties below grass
amassing armored masses to fight red on black for world control
from a twig to the outer territories by the far fence post.

Following the brain in its baggy elliptical flow to the corner store
past open house notices, aren't I supposed to do more than notice
that the world is fizzling out and even find some kind of order,
a pattern in the hand signals leaves make in breeze?
Or, tell me the truth, Henry, is that schizophrenic?
I think I see a design in buckled sidewalk, but how to decipher
the circle round the "K," the bell that rings when I step inside,
the silent rows of Snickers, mounds of Mounds, the sour Zours?

Blow your tiny horns, insect trumpeters! Let all the popcorns
pop at once, the girly mags drop off the walls, the grey matter rip
with electricity! No, I think I'll just go back to drowsing about
and looking for snacks. What else can I do when it's beyond my ken
—the way the unclosed "P" on the handwritten sign
on the TIPS jar makes me think of TITS, the five-buck bill
I drop thoughtless into the jar and my goofy smile
fading inside the tired girl behind the counter, chewing gum?

Parable of the Gifts

For her birthday I bought eight small gifts, a silver pen with rubber grip, a silver hair clip, a silver Zippo lighter on which I had engraved *You are a poem*. A glass and silver box within which were seven smaller glass and silver boxes. A lavender and olive oil soap bar, a lavender mist, a lavender and aloe hand lotion. And other gifts, all lavender and silver, each in its own small box, wrapped in hand-made paper, with ribbons, bows, and loving notes. And what made it better was that it all cost too much and we were much too poor, so how she'd love me more when I pulled out each new gift we couldn't afford.

I gave the soap when she woke up, the lotion over coffee, and saved the rest for other meals, for with the cake, and on the dance floor, and before bed. And right before we left to meet our friends she called out, "Take the garbage," which I did, the five white bags laid by the door, and walked them to the dumpster, then went back for our bags. And now you know the rest. Of course I'd thrown the presents out, and of course, when I ran out the garbage truck had just left with the presents nestled in its belly.

And we jumped into the car and raced around the neighborhood until we found the truck, and I leapt out and convinced the nice garbage men to let me climb into that underworld in my dress shoes and pants and dig. Inside the truck, up to my knees in muck, while the garbage men looked on and lent me gloves and their advice, I lifted stinking paper bags, newspapers and broken toys, and tossed them in a whirl of flies and anger for an hour, until, exhausted, I sat down in the garbage and breathed it in, the smell of my own failure.

And now each time I pass the Dumpster I say *Oh*, and look inside, as if the cosmos might take pity and the gifts appear, as if the cosmos practiced recycling, and why not? —Adam made from clay and Eve from bone, Lazarus brought back from death, the Jewish rabbi dead and then reborn, stranger things have happened, or so they say. But no, they don't come back. And though the woman who was then my wife forgave me the second I climbed down the ladder into that world of trash, it took me longer to accept. At first I took some comfort in the notion of the presents waiting in their boxes underground for some future exhumation. But later I gave up on that illusion, gave in and knew that though they went astray, the nature of the gifts is that they're given, and given away.

Parable of Riding a Motorcycle Off a Cliff

"A man falls from his chariot. His bones are the same
as everyone else's, but his injury is different."
—Chuang Tzu

When his back wheel fishtails, time goes
sideways, so he has time to see each bright
pine needle on which the oil-black tires slide,
time to note the white curb, knuckle skin
tightening as his hand clenches on the brake,
time to know he has no time for anything
but smack the curb sideways and tumble,
or angle the bike straight and hurdle the curb
into the unknown, which is what he does.
But he flies between pines and doesn't clip them,
and it rained last night so the ground he hits
is moist and soft, and he goes dead but wakes up bloody
and shoves the fractured bike off his girlfriend,
who hasn't figured so far in this story,
but who is wearing a helmet and survives just fine,
and then they walk back to her apartment,
and her roommates bring a warm wet towel
to wash blood and mud from his face, "But wait,"
he says, "let's take a photo first. This is a moment
I want to remember." Twenty years later, after he fell
for another woman he didn't figure on putting
into this story, the snapshot drops from a book
he unpacks from a box while moving into his new place,
his new life after his life with her went crash.

He picks it up off the floor, an old black and white
of some leather-jacketed young guy, full of beginnings,
with a black blood smudge running from his nose,
some fool staring out of the past, grinning.

Psalm of Speed

The man in the next car screams into his beard,
bashing fists against the leather wheel,
but traffic has the ancient indifference of the universe,
which carries on its ordinary chaos with no theory,
intelligence, or design, and I think of it as slowly forever
rippling away from some original big blast
like the tidal wave of boiling molasses that rolled
through Boston, 1919, when the high sun swelled it
till the great tank burst, cooking and drowning
the people in the street or sweeping them into the Bay.
On display in my own glass case, I think, *Get Zen,*
get Zen like a mindless cloud carried on a wind,
like that old haiku: *Climb Mt. Fuji, O snail, slowly, slowly.*

Whatever speed we go, the past keeps passing into the past,
though years ago when I was married and saw the years
opening before me like rooms in a pleasure palace,
I'd corkscrew helmetless through traffic on my motorcycle,
savage with speed, while people at a dead stop watched
through windowshields and maybe that's why
when we rented a dune buggy on the island of Naxos
and drove eroded roads to see the reclining kouros
in a garden hung with jasmine and hibiscus,
the woman behind the counter sized me up and told me
in thick English, "Go slowly, slowly, honking a lot."

Now around me the motorcycles weave free while slowly
I nose towards the source of trouble, black smoke flung into sky
like crows fleeing a burning barn, while below flames fly
forty feet high from a blazing truck canted on its side.
Slowly, slowly, we pass it by, each of us studying
what could have happened to us on the road,
and some of us are happy enough that the big burn
is still around some other turn, while others scream behind glass,
honking a lot, then hit the gas, swerve onto the shoulder
and speed away from it, spitting gravel, as fast as fast.

Discourse on the Tao of Shoe Shopping

The perfect man's mind is like a mirror
in which the ten thousand things pass
without taking hold, and from my perspective
in the shoe store mirror the world is simplified
to shins and knees jackknifing past.
At another angle, in another low mirror, the traffic
is just shivering hips and lithe thighs.
Crotches scrunched up in blue jeans
and asses flexing in stretchy skirts pass
like the scraps of conversation flowing through me.
And I feel the eyes on my neck and back:
strange guy in a leather coat scribbling fiercely
on the back flyleaf of a book of bad poems.
What's he doing in here? The shop girl considers me
uncertainly, but I don't look up, I just write this
quickly, a life sketch snatched out of the current
before my wife comes up to me, says, "Let's go,
there's nothing here," and I stand up, thinking
about perspective, about my body bent
on this wooden bench and then unbent
so when I glance back at the floor mirror
I see just shoes going past, flat sole, square-toed,
cork bottom, kid leather, boot-soled, leopard skin,
and the ankles, bony, skins stretched tight,
those sweet hinges linking moment to moment
flex and release, release and flex.

Parable of Greece, Grasshopper, Time

Everything tumbles forward end-over-end
like a stone down a mountain.
He keeps waking up (it's a pinprick,
like the mosquito that bit him on the neck
just now) and then forgetting again.
Just now, for instance, his wife
walks in the door from washing
her bathing suit and gives a little shriek:
a very large grasshopper has bounced through
the open door and crouches on the floor
near the computer cord, about to leap.
"Get out! Get out! You stupid grasshopper,
I'm going to have to kill you,"
she whispers, trying not to disturb him
as he writes, urging the grasshopper
toward the door with a flyswatter.
One thing, then another.
Now, for instance, his brother is at the door,
come to take them dancing at the port.
He has to stop writing this.
His wife says, "Rob says you have to come
right now." And now, for instance,
he comes back years later to revise this poem,
and wonders if he should take out
words that no longer apply, such as
"his wife." Here's what gets him:
how it never stops, world after world,
how he keeps falling through.

Testament of the Oldest White Belt at the Tae Kwon Do Tournament

And, as the fight goes on for centuries, a whole Middle Ages of creaky tendons, shoulder pain and faulty prostates, Dark Age of crusades and iron maidens and the always-present threat of the Black Death, what's to come seems no better, inquisitions and pogroms and the death of God, but still he's kicking back with dead-weight legs, trying to get in combos, to breathe, dodge or even just keep his fists up, and he does, though it hurts, he kicks death right in her narrow black teeth,

because instead of resting his face against the kitchen linoleum and wanting to die, staring at the dead ants below the refrigerator, after the divorce he learned how to fight in matches that have done something to time, so they don't seem to end, like the longest sentence in the world, punctuated with elbowed shins, kicked wrists and rib-kicks, fighting other dudes with something to prove, who hit him so hard their fists rip skin right through foam arm guards, they donkey-kick the breath out of him, exhaust themselves on his body, they're picturing their boss' face and tacking it over his, kicking at their guts and hair plugs and ex-loves,

and after the fight, his throat harsh from hard breathing, he's dying-hot in thick chest pads, shaking on his feet as he bows to the judges, his wrists feel rickety, and he winces when his girlfriend grabs him by the biceps, groans when she pats his sore left buttock, and deep bone bruises surface a week later, lemon-colored and the size and shape of peaches or rubber bullets or closed fists, muted suns on arms and shins, these strange blood oranges, burning under the skin as he walks around hemorrhaging fresh pain, somewhat alive.

Gospel of the Famous Heart

The artist who tried to get the museum to display a white, used urinal is dead. But that urinal into which so many pent-up souls released, went on show, signed, labeled, non-odorific and dry. So we turn into art. Maybe living's a kind of art? Maybe I could remove this thing from its bone cage, and send it freeze-dried to the New York Society of Independent Artists, labeled "My Heart," but then I'd need a replacement. In China they think the brain's the seat of passion, not the heart, but since this is America I could shop for one at Oh My Heart down at the medical mall, steel hearts with plastic valves, stainless and digitally regular, porcelain hearts with rubber aortas, pretty but easily shattered, even flesh hearts like clenched fists, that old technology the salesman steers me away from while looking askance at the moist chamber open in my chest. Meanwhile, back in my life, I've survived the divorce, though it still bites when I read my old poems and have to say words that have ceased to pertain, such as "My Wife."

She had it tough deciding whether to love me or not, like that artist who designed his Paris apartment so the front entrance and the bathroom shared one door—she hinged back-and-forth, stay-or-leave, duty-passion-friendship-sex for years, and when she finally went I felt all my futures had slammed shut, latched, locked, bolted and barred, but tried to live with an open heart, and wrote it down to control the hurt, open-and-shut, open-and-shut, as long as the valves do that I'll stay alive, wet, cherry-red and pumping. You want to see my drained grey heart behind glass like a skinned dove? I'm sorry, it's my birthday and a woman wearing red lingerie has just come into the room, and I'm getting distracted. I love her, she is shaking her heart-shaped ass at me and she says, "Come out of your head!" And you, reading this poem, you don't get to join us in bed, where liquid yellow candlelight shivers on two bodies hinging open-and-shut, pulse at the neck, red tongues—it's my birthday, not yours, the door is locked, and you are standing outside, paparazzi at an opening, hoping to catch a glimpse of the famous heart.

The Miniature Vedas

On Failure

She says, "I think I *could*
be anorexic. I just don't have
the discipline.

ఌ

Economy

She reserves
her nastiest digs
for the man she loves.

ఌ

A Grimm Tale

Once upon a time
she loved him. Then
she just fucking stopped.

ఌ

Bastards

Revenge on the road.
Not worth it
in gun country.

Coincidence

The first time I dropped acid,
she said, was also, as it turned out,
the first time I had anal sex.

୭

"The Kalahari Kung

only have sex every five years,"
she said, "so don't tell me
you *need* sex."

୭

What His Girlfriend Said While They Made Love

"I know what you did, you ate onions."
"And you didn't?" He asked.
"No, fucker," she said. "I don't eat onions."

୭

I Feel like Jesus Crucified, He Said,

as she dangled her breasts in his face
and pinned his wrists to the sheets.
"Yeah," she said, "Only better."

"I Feel Fortunate to Experience You,"

she said as he rubbed passion fruit lotion
on her breasts, "in this window of time
when you are a free little slut."

§

Angry

at his parents,
he snaps the neck
of his own guitar.

§

Greek Ruins

Looking up through the streets of Athens,
the boy cries, "Look!
You can see the Apocalypse!"

§

Arranging Driftwood into Sculpture,

the boy is concentrated as a fist.
When he walks down to the water's edge,
it reverts to junk.

There's Something So Sad

about one shoe left by the roadside.
But underwear left at the beach,
that's just funny.

᭓

On Translating Chinese Sex Manuals

"At last," Bob tells me,
"You have some research
that will keep you up at night."

᭓

The Poem He Thought of

while falling asleep;
maybe he'll remember it
in a dream.

᭓

In His Dream He Sees an Ancient Japanese Knife,

and on it, written, DEATH.
Now that would be a hell
of a knife to cook with.

In the Morning

before coffee,
he tries to shave
with his toothbrush.

§

What's Next?

Wakes up one day,
his shoulder no longer moves.
Doctor says, "It happens."

§

"One Good Thing about Divorce," She Said,

"I get to stop
being a character
in your damn poems."

Parable of the Incredible Shrinking Man

The boyfriend starts out large in her mind, and so it takes a while to slice
him to the right size. She starts with a small scalpel to score his skin,
practice cuts to mark the places she will later swing the bone-and-
flesh-hacking machete she keeps inside her purse. Of course
you think of that tavern owner who would chop a traveler's
legs off if they did not fit his bed, but soon the boyfriend
is too small to sleep with in the bed, not just because
his penis pokes like a skinny finger in her ribs. If
she rolls at night she'll crush him. So she
moves him to the cat cage, feeding him
warm milk with nippled
droppers at which
he gratefully
sucks.

Later she keeps him in a stew pot lined with papers, peering in
to see him run in frantic circles like a gerbil. He's too minute
to complain, shrinking until he is this tiny bit of flesh
coiled 'round her finger, desperately grasping his
own ankles—an itty-bitty man she just wants to
shake off, to fling him in the trash and walk
away while from the promontory of an
orange peel above the stony beach of
coffee grounds he calls after
her giant retreating form
with piercing, tiny,
horror movie
screams.

American Ramayana

Even after he's reborn into another life, it makes a skunkweed
whiff of pot shoot up the nose like wasabi to hear "Mellissa,"
and "Rambling Man" evokes that after-party smell of smoke
and beer-vomit in the carpets. In those years in the hairy Midwest,
when men wore moustaches like porn stars or desperados
and women were demons with feathered hair and blue-painted eyes and red claws,
he was known as the party king in his pleasure palace
in the woods, where knackered guests would fling
themselves from the third floor balcony on a rope swing, scream
into the darkness between trees, then run upstairs to fly again.

But the kingdom was brought down for the love of the girl
they nicknamed Sexy Sadie, with skin like molten silver, large eyes
kohled and moist, hair like clustered dates, breasts that leapt
like deer—in dreams, though in the daytime she was dirty blonde
and ordinary, but with a poet's soul, and gentle, and smarter than the rest,
and not in love with him. To be alive and in this life was like rubbing
a needle against his eye, and a part of him went dead,
his soul was rotten flesh, his heart was clammy wet, and his penis
stung him like a barb stuck in his groin, and so he drove
his rusted truck that leaked exhaust into the cab and sold hard water
stain remover in Lodi, and hustled pool in Santa Cruz,
and lost his stake in a card room in Bakersfield and went at last
to wander in the demon forest with sages and with imps.
When he came into the world again with matted muddy locks
he was as different from his old self as a sandal is from mud,
an elephant from a cat, a bong hit from cocaine, he was reborn
like an Indian god, wielding a bow with terrible black arrows
carved with sutras that darted hissing through the air, tipped

with heads of falcons, boars and sea monsters, and burning
with phosphorus and starlight and whipping ponytails of flame.

And now he lived in a hippie town by the coast with tattoo parlors
and pool halls and sour, trust-fund punks with death-faces and metal-
pierced skin, their hair aflame. They crushed the gorgeous grass
into the earth with great black boots of their despair and tried to wreck
the cars their parents bought them, but he lived in a flophouse
by the sports bar, with a Vietnam Vet who took a Skilsaw
to the drywall and the door of his room when he moved out,
and his chariot was a motorcycle and his armor was a leather jacket
and he was beautiful and he was poor. That was when he met
his love, and she had long hair clustered like dark grapes, and skin
like molten gold, lips like cherries, breasts like etcetera,
and she loved him until she didn't. She loved him
and she married him and they lived a lifetime till she left.
That's when he cast himself into the village well and in the dark
he turned to meat, just tendons, muscles and an outside envelope
of moist cuticle and porous skin, all nails and teeth and urine
and bile, attracting cockroaches and tiny black goblins.

Yet what crawled up from the well was an even greater god,
with lightning in his hair, a tornado in his mind, and a tongue
that gilded the world with yellow light. He lived now in the suburbs,
shopped at Trader Joe's, shedding blessing and psalms, and his students
prayed to him, and he was alive. That was when an illusion
rose out of the desert like a woman with a white deer neck,
her hair like red dates braided in clusters below her waist.

She was the young gazelle of the tribe, her face like the bright cloak
of the sun, her breasts like polished mirrors reflecting his desire
and what was worse for him the desire of every other man
who sat inside his empty tent, plotting. She had lips like rubies,
teeth like whatever, a mind like a beehive, full of secret
dark motion, and she imagined she could tame each bad
and pretty man. When she asked would he watch the child
and dog and buy her ticket to the next city, he said, "Of course!"
And she went to see a tall man from the other tribe,
who found sport in stealing in and sneaking the goddess off
to his bed where he pinned her down and fucked
the pictures in his head that she resembled.

And so he lost a second family in one life, and lay in bed till noon,
and fell to the carpet crying, "Oh!" and called her slut and bitch and whore
and punched himself in the face and heart, and when he stood
before the tribunal and when his heart was taken from its cage
and weighed against a feather on the scales he swore he loved her
when she sneered at him, loved her when she raged, loved her failure
to stay in love because it made her perfection human.
That was when something crawled in upon a lion stomach,
foreclaws of a crocodile, and great gray hindparts of a hippopotamus.
Hearing noise behind, he asked, "Have you come back?"
but no, it was a monster from the book of imaginary beings,
imaginary as the god who said, *Worship me and live a full life*
in an empty world, imaginary as this love masticated by time.
It was the Devourer of the Dead. It gobbled up his heart
weighed down with grief. It left him standing by the television,
bathed in light, with a hole inside his chest, turning blue.

Turtle Head Psalm

—for Gerald Stern

I'm thinking of the woman who left me, her angry redhead beauty,
her combustion engine of a soul, her flaming petroleum sex,
thinking of our first night kissing all night on the couch
and it makes me think of all that weird Chinese pornography
brushed out by horny Mandarins in sexy calligraphy,
and I have to ask why? Why the peony flower and not
the rhododendron with its hot pink folds, why not the tulip
with its polished red skin, not the lily with its purple pursed lips?

And why did the African prostitutes in red spandex shorts
on the night streets of Athens beneath the great white bones
of the Acropolis look at me with that knowing look in their eyes?
What did they know of the young French novelist I was with,
too young for me, it's true, who doesn't like making love from behind
even when we are kissing, but I like it, damn me, the making love
from behind and the kissing, and does that make me bad?
The pimp in the doorway and the African prostitutes
in red spandex shorts make me think of Confucius who said,
if he ever lived, that beautiful old fart, who said, "I've never met a man
who cares about ethics as much as he cares about sex."

It's true that when I close my eyes I see the parts of the body
in astrological conjunction and it makes me think
about all that weird Chinese pornography, with the man's jade
stalk sinking deep into the dew-covered peony flower, and the man
like some kind of vampire sucking the woman's *chi* into himself
through the great curved fang of his penis, trying to retain his semen
because to orgasm which we call to *come* but some cultures call to *go*

for the Chinese means to *spend,* so that after sex you are *spent*
if you allow your great snapping turtle head to spout out its
silver stream, its river of plasma, its Milky Way wonders.

Spent, the way I felt before I met my French novelist,
though walking the streets of Athens I'm still wondering:
why all this friction of skin leads to oxytocin fictions of love,
that physical affliction of dopamine release, the opiate addiction,
the chemicals in the brain? Is it all in the way we name it? Humping
or making love? Jade stalk, turtle head, monk's bald pate and vertical flute
but not the bamboo fighting pole, neck of the reticulated giraffe,
the hairy spitting camel or the swaying upright cobra? Whatever
we call it I still felt spent thinking about the woman who left me,
her angry intelligence, oh smarter than me, I'm happy
to admit it, and stronger as well, strong enough to walk away,
though it was a short walk into another man's bed,
less faithful than me, but then who isn't?

And does this make me a jerk, to be writing about these women,
though one of them pleaded, *Don't make me famous?*
Does it make me a jerk to write about Sarah,
whom I knew in China when I was twenty-four
with hair and muscles and shyness and a few poems
shining in green pixels on my tiny computer screen?
Sarah a debutante from Georgia who gave me the Asian clap
and gave it as well to two Chinese poets, so when my sister called,
her voice electric in the long transpacific cable from California,
and asked *What shall I bring you when I come,* I said
A medium-sized diaphragm and three doses of penicillin,

because I had awakened with blood in my underwear,
blood in my sheets, the turtle head was spitting red
and all because she had white skin, as white as tree grubs,
that's what the Chinese would say, she had great swaying breasts,
like lard the Chinese would say, smooth thighs like jade
and nipples like comets, a brain like a rose, many-petaled
and sweet, dethorned, oh and a welcoming vagina,
can I write that or does it make me an asshole to say, a
welcoming tongue, a soul I could love, her artist soul
I rode her body trying to penetrate through to.

Oh Sarah, in relative time and space you are lost now absolutely
but still in the past our ghosts are rocking on the bed,
bicycling together, turtles climbing into each other's shells,
flowers kissing flowers, our ghosts are living still like
the billions of dead Chinese, the girl embryos scraped out
of the womb, the Boxers shot down by the British,
ghosting like women who wrote poems to each other
in a secret language, poems they loved so much
they had them placed upon their chests beneath folded hands
in the coffin, food for twisting hungry worms,
and all of us rotting underneath the dirt of time, all rising
like wine fumes from a shattered glass, the novelist
and the bad lover and Sarah and the prostitutes who know
as they see us walking down the street holding hands
that the restaurant we are looking for has long ago closed.

Psalm of Snow

I had forgotten how to say *yes*. That's the trick of heartbreak.
It makes you forget *yes*. The voices in my head were not kind,
so you took me to the woods to empty out.
My old shoulder was wired with pain, and there was a needle
in my hip, but we lay on a wide flat rock in the snow
as the intoxicated sun licked our faces with breathing light

like a yellow dog, simple in its joy, licking our chins and lips and necks
and a long wind came from over the mountaintop
and cooled our left sides, and the Sacramento River
wept through us like time, and spoke its liquid foolish syllables,
senseless, sensual, almost sentient, and I lay with my head
nested between your breasts and listened.

Time to climb, you said, and I felt snow-wing angelic as we snowshoed
above Castle Lake, leaving traces behind like snow rabbits
with webbed feet, silver squirrels, prints on the glass of the world,
a little evidence for angels to investigate after that death magic
resolves us to nothing again. I heard omens in the wind, psalms
in the bent warm sunlight that makes the snow mountains weep.

Something was coming, something foreign as joy, a clue
to how to live once you're done with sorrow, a way of being
in being like a long breath exhaled, leaving a trace on the air
before it resolves again to air, the frozen lake, ice fishers waiting
for something great to rise, the mountaintop lifting
its white head in trance and saying its one good word: snow.

Biographical Note

Tony Barnstone is Professor of English at Whittier College and has a Masters in English and Creative Writing and Ph.D. in English Literature from UC Berkeley. His other books of poems include *Sad Jazz: Sonnets* (Sheep Meadow Press, 2005) and *Impure: Poems by Tony Barnstone* (University Press of Florida, 1998) in addition to the chapbook *Naked Magic* (Main Street Rag). He is also a distinguished translator of Chinese poetry and literary prose and an editor of literary textbooks. His books in these areas include *Chinese Erotic Poetry* (Everyman, 2007); *The Anchor Book of Chinese Poetry* (Anchor, 2005); *Out of the Howling Storm: The New Chinese Poetry* (Wesleyan, 1993); *Laughing Lost in the Mountains: Poems of Wang Wei* (UP of New England, 1991); *The Art of Writing: Teachings of the Chinese Masters* (Shambhala, 1996); and the textbooks *Literatures of Asia, Africa and Latin America, Literatures of Asia,* and *Literatures of the Middle East* (all from Prentice Hall Publishers). He is the recipient of many national poetry prizes and of fellowships from the National Endowment for the Arts and the California Arts Council. Born in Middletown, Connecticut, and raised in Bloomington, Indiana, Barnstone has lived in Greece, Spain, Kenya and China.